Stacy A. Cross is an American Author, Entrepreneur, Life Coach and Inspirational Speaker. Stacy A. Cross is known for her no-holds barred communication style and her passion for helping others reach their full potential in life, work, and business.

She is the founder of The Comfort Killers, one of the fastest-growing self-improvement and coaching companies and groups today. Through The Comfort Killers brand, Stacy A. Cross challenges her readers, viewers, and listeners to step outside of their comfort zone in order to achieve their dreams.

Stacy has worked and created content with beautiful minds inside and outside of business such as:

- Grant Cardone - NY Times Best Selling Author, International Speaker, Real Estate Investor, and Sales Trainer.
- Kevin Harrington - Founder of "As Seen On TV," and Original Shark on Television Series Shark Tank.
- Billy Shaw Gene – Entrepreneur and Digital Marketing Expert.
- Gordon Bizar – Entrepreneur, business coach, finance adviser, mentor and educator.
- Many more.

For a full catalog of The Comfort Killers visit the YouTube channel
https://www.youtube.com/thecomfortkillers

TABLE OF CONTENTS

THE COMFORT KILLERS

YOUR JOURNEY TO SUCCESS:

How to Change Your Life Using Tools You Already Have

By

Stacy A. Cross

Edited by Anthony Infantino
Cover art by James Spooner
Inside illustration by Joe Smith

Published by The Comfort Killers LLC
www.thecomfortkillers.com

ISBN 978-0-692-08930-9

EK COMFORT KILLERS®
YOUR JOURNEY TO SUCCESS

FORWARD

I had the privilege of discovering Stacy Cross approximately a year and a half ago. I was initially drawn to Stacy's energy shown daily in her motivating tweets. In an age where many "Self Help Gurus" offer "5 Steps to Relaxation" and "10 Steps to Make Work Easier," Stacy was advocating a different approach—finding and eliminating the areas of Comfort in one's life. This approach was so radically different that it shook me to my core and forced me to challenge many perceptions I had regarding my own life.

I can attest to the fact that Stacy lives daily the principles she preaches to her ever-growing number of "Comfort Killers." I have worked with many passionate leaders and dedicated individuals. I have not met someone more driven in sharing the techniques of personal development than Stacy Cross.

Read this book and think about the principles. More importantly, take action in utilizing those principles today.

~ *James F. Flanagan Co-founder of The Comfort Killers*

****

First, I want to thank you for beginning your journey as a Comfort Killer. Stacy created this book so you can start where you are, right now. No excuses. Start today.

The reason you are reading this book is because, honestly, being a Comfort Killer is something that is in all of us. However, society unfortunately conditions us to suppress and silence our natural instinct to be a Comfort Killer. But that stops now.

Over the last year of knowing Stacy and being a part of the Comfort Killers, I have noticed change within myself. Little by little, I can see and feel myself evolving and improving. But it takes action. Daily action.

This is where most individuals lose on their journey to success. They are not able to commit to daily action. Let's be honest. We have all been there, we all get stuck, we all get misguided, and we all are distracted.

But losing is not an option, because you have the guide and information to make change with what you have now! No more ingredients are necessary!

One thing I know is that your mindset will change after you fully engage in the contents of this book. The pages that follow are lined with real information, no fluff. The steps you need to get uncomfortable and prosper on your journey to success. One thing about Stacy and about being a Comfort Killer: there is no fluff, no fakery, just 100% pure grade-A material.

But let me warn you! If you are interested in a magical fairy tale scenario, this book may not be of the upmost benefit to you. This is for those that want freedom and success but know that there will be grit and grind associated. This is for the individuals that understand that comfort must become a thing of the past.

What will be your story? What will be your legacy? What is your destination on this journey to success? What will you be willing to give up? And how far will you go to attain everything that you want?

The best thing about the questions above is that you are in control of the answers. It's your time, and you are in control—all of your answers require you getting uncomfortable. Thankfully you have within you everything you need to succeed. This book will provide you methods and techniques on how to activate these tools.

~ *Thelonious C. Jones, Real Estate Investor and Solutionist*

****

Being a part of The Comfort Killers and bearing witness to Stacy's personal journey has been inspiring, to say the least. Believe it or not, Stacy and I met in elementary school. Many years later we reconnected. This time around I was working two jobs and entering the first semester of my Master's program. She was between jobs but had recently accepted an offer from an airline. While our lives were in very different places, we were able to find time to get to know each other and begin our journey. Stacy was good at so many things. I was always amazed by her talents. She loved music, computers, technology, and her family. She also told me about another passion of hers, a clothing brand she had been working on. I had even seen her help people with their college coursework. She was extremely resourceful, yet she was battling something much bigger, I was so wrapped up with my own stuff it took me almost two years to realize ... she was addicted to gambling.

I'll be honest, this was not an addiction that I had ever had any personal experience with. I'm from New Jersey, going to casinos in Atlantic City was something my family and friends did for fun. We laughed on the way in and laughed on the way out. With Stacy it was different. I could barely keep up with her once we walked in. As we grew closer the severity of the situation grew more apparent, the gambling was taking over. Fast forward as we approach year five of the relationship, I told myself I would not deal with this another year. I tried all the methods I knew of to help, without success. She was not aware of my promise to myself, but she knew she had a problem and was determined to be her true self and shine bright.

I witnessed Stacy literally change her life. This was a rare sight; many people do not make the drastic steps on their own to really bring them out of dark places. She began to use different methods to change her thought process, her mindset. She was reading more, exercising, and taking a hard look at what got her where she was. She took personal development to a whole other level. It required commitment, daily commitment. A year later I was looking at someone who had not stepped foot into a casino, someone who had become more responsible, someone who found the solutions and got uncomfortable and created The

Comfort Killers. She used all her experiences, good and bad, and was beginning to help others realize their own potential daily. I was one of those people. Even before Stacy moved into this new time in her life, she was always supportive and encouraged me to do what was best for myself. The knowledge, wisdom and resources she shared through her business allowed me, not only to take a role in the business and be a part of so many great moments, but catapulted me into starting my own business. In two years I went from an hour and a half commute to work to being self-employed and building my own brand. The confidence to do this all stemmed from being a Comfort Killer. In six and a half years we helped each other climb to new heights, a priceless adventure that lead to a friendship that will last a lifetime.

This book will give you the tools, resources, and steps you need to move into the life you want, help you get uncomfortable, and to live *your* definition of success in life and in business.

~ Shivhon Adkins, Founder of Medical Receptionist Network (and my best friend)

GIVE ME 30 DAYS

... and I Guarantee YOUR Life Will Change

"Discover The Amazing Success Formula That Even A Lazy, Unmotivated, and Undisciplined Individual Can Use To Completely Turn Their Life Around in 30 Days ...Guaranteed!"

I share with you 30+ techniques you can use one day at a time, without getting overwhelmed and overloaded- which in the past, is the <u>ONLY</u> reason you quit.

The Comfort Killers Building Blocks to Success 30-Day Program is different. I take time delivering each tool, technique and resource while <u>automatically</u> and subconsciously reinforcing each success building block over the course of 30 days without too much input from you.

The best part about it is ... **YOU CHOOSE** what is <u>working for you</u> and continue with it. The better you feel about yourself, the higher your self-worth, <u>the more likely you will achieve success.</u>

Do you want more love, money, happiness, abundance, peace and fruitful relationships?

If You Answered YES ...
Then You Are Ready For This Program

Since you've already taken massive ACTION by purchasing a copy of this book, **I am GIVING you my KILLER program for Free ($997.00 VALUE).** This offer is only valid for a limited time so head over to the website below and SIGN UP NOW!

www.HowToGetUncomfortable.com

WHAT IS A COMFORT KILLER?

I created this bad-ass company as a way for me to overcome a gambling addiction I carried with me for 9 years and grow into a person of interest. Basically, I used it as my vehicle to success. It was harsh, and at first I didn't quite understand the value of it—I just knew I was fed up with being controlled by the slot machines, craps table, and the almighty dollar.

I already had a podcast called "Get Uncomfortable" that I hosted during my time starting a clothing brand called Preferred Classics. I loved the name, but at that time it was never tied to anything other than me trying to figure out how this mindset thing worked and how it could possibly be changed. Little by little it came to me that my true purpose was not to deliver t-shirts and socks, but instead, use my energy and voice to help millions get uncomfortable to live better lives.

So, there I was—year 2016—in debt, broke, and broken with minimal self-confidence, energy, and self-esteem. I was at my lowest point—I was at zero. I wanted to do things differently, so I signed up to a bunch of free seminars to meet new people, maybe make some new friends, and learn about what had been holding me back. Little did I know, it was me the entire time.

Like it was yesterday, I remember walking into this seminar all dressed up to learn about wealth and entrepreneurship. Immediately, I met a young man—a man who is still a good friend of mine to this day—and introduced myself. He explained that he was a business consultant and was working on a few projects. He handed me his awesome, well-designed business card and he asked for mine. I had nothing to give him in return. I told him to just give me his number; I would plug it in my phone. His name was Richard Sutton, now speaker and author of *Fear of Becoming a Man*, and a great inspiration to many in the community. He didn't know it then, and probably doesn't know it now, but he changed my entire path by asking me one question: "What do you do?" I thought to myself whether it would be appropriate to say I have a podcast only or if I should say I am starting a business. I had previously shut down my clothing brand, Preferred Classics, a few months before we met. I surely couldn't use that as something I did. It was then that something inside me found its way to my consciousness and voiced out "I am a Comfort Killer, and I host the 'Get Uncomfortable Podcast Show.'" Richard's eyes lit up. I struck something inside him. I could tell. Was it the name? Was it how confident I said it? I didn't know. All I did know was that I needed a pen and paper quick because I needed to remember the name: The Comfort Killers. That was the first time I ever said it. It was the inception of something greater than myself. It was energy. Was it an accident?

I ran the hell out of the seminar rejuvenated, bursting with life, love, and power. Before the seminar was over, I shook my new friend Richard Sutton's hands and ran out because I knew that my mission was bigger than that room. I couldn't have explained it at that point in time, how powerful it was feeling energized to a point it over-powered my mind and body. Using this power, I was able to overcome gambling addiction. The addiction was instantly redirected as I set out on my new journey. I would be destined to create a company that teaches millions how to get uncomfortable, to think better, act better, and live better.

This book is the product and result of the same energy that I will teach you how to create at will. It is already inside of you, awaiting activation. You will learn how to sum up lost powers inside you and take control of your life. This book is about changing the direction of your life in such a way that others may find you crazy, weird and beautifully renewed. It doesn't matter really what anyone thinks. It just matters how you feel. If you are producing great things, you feel good. When you are producing below average products or results, you feel bad. I want you to feel good, because it's natural. Things flow to you better when you produce good in the world.

This book will be your life guide. You should read it once, then read it again, and then on the 3rd time, you will have understood everything. Then read it again in a year. Let me remind you that this is not about racing. This is about taking drastic steps to better your circumstances. You will more than likely have a reduced text log— because you will be too focused on yourself. People will begin to ask you, "Yo! Why aren't you at the Sunday Night Football party anymore?" You won't even answer. You will find that things are just not as important anymore. They will not stimulate you. You will begin to set your own path—one in which you are the creator, owner, founder, CEO, and leader. A path you are the source of. You will start to think differently, then suddenly, your stance and behaviors change —later your whole damn life will be different. It's real. It happened to me, and it has been an amazing journey ever since.

Don't resist change especially when you are so close to it. It's already happening as soon as you grab for a book like this. You ask or you saw and looked around and said: "WTF is a Comfort Killer!!!?" When you ask the right questions, the answer will soon materialize.

Yes—I teach people how to improve themselves. How to get better at communication. How to progress through life. How to leave the bullshit at the door and take responsibility. All of this I teach. But I cannot teach you how to want it. You must already want it. You must already have been asking yourself questions. I literally am here because you asked for it. Nothing more, nothing less. But don't ever question what you have created. Just know that I am here because of you. Period!

So, what is a Comfort Killer? You will soon learn about who we are, but first, you must be 100% open to taking action after reading this book. We eat, breathe, and bleed action. In my next book, I will talk about developing your entrepreneurial mindset, creating a business, and maximizing your investments because you'll get to a point on your journey where it makes sense to take your next step to success. That's the next book. In this book, we will change our behaviors, and that's that! Here is my disclaimer. I am not a psychologist. I prescribe new ways of thinking deliberately throughout this entire thing, which aren't really new at all. You already have all the resources you need inside you. This book will help you raise your consciousness so that you can see them. Be sure to use everything you need while you are reading this book. I want you to EAT this book. Write notes, highlight, underline, circle words, and really OWN this book. Just do whatever works for you. It's all about doing the opposite, more on that a little later.

One thing to know about The Comfort Killers is that we are a community of alternative thinkers. We want data that helps us. We are not into the gimmicks or short-lived flow. We are focused on real growth and real results. There will be people that you come across on this journey that will be pulling your strings more than wanting to support you. You will be able to spot them and spit them out without thinking twice about it. This journey is uncomfortable and a whole lot will be coming your way super quick, and you must not give up what YOU wanted in the first place—to change your damn life!

WELCOME TO *THE COMFORT KILLERS*

Qualities of a Comfort Killer

There are qualities that we must aim to dress ourselves in that will become a habit and will make up our character and personality. We will wear these new qualities like articles of clothing and remember that we are acting 'as if' before it becomes part of who we are. We must learn to be good at improve which is defined as a theatrical technique, before we see these changes in our qualities and before they can become habitual. Did you know the definition of "habit" as a transitive verb is "clothe" or "dress?" The reason I know this is because I have a nasty habit of looking words up using a dictionary and also going as far as searching for the etymology of a word. I suggest you get into this nasty little habit too. It's great to know what words meant before we diluted them with years and years of conventional wisdom. When you create a new habit, you clothe yourself with it. Picture yourself putting on a new and improved habit and walk out the door like you are earning this year's Tony Award. It's as easy as choosing who you want to become, then play that role. Let's play a game.

Below is a list of qualities that makes one a Comfort Killer:

- Courageous
- Self-motivated
- Different
- Risk taker
- Leader
- Resilient
- Creative
- Top performer
- Unwilling to take no for an answer

- Strong belief in oneself
- Willing to go above and beyond all the time
- OK with criticism
- Not content with traditional thinking
- Assertive
- Goal oriented
- Unafraid to stand for beliefs
- Living outside of the comfort zone

This is who we are. We can adopt as many of these qualities as we want. There's no one stopping us. The only one stopping you from changing your life is you.

Let's first define what improvisation is according to *Merriam-Webster Dictionary*; it is "the act or art of improvising." How does one act out being creative? What does one do? Well, first one must act as if one is already creative before the actual doing part.

You can say things like "I Am creative." This affirmation is to yourself. You can post it everywhere. You are already creative. In the next subchapter, you will learn how to find others who are already creative and peel away at their life and take what you want. It's that simple, just adopt the individual's quality and apply it to your life.

All that is left is you proclaiming that you are creative. You are already a beautiful creative being. Everything you want is already inside of you. Let's take a moment and define the word you wish to become. Grab your dictionary. Just to forewarn you, you will be needing a dictionary to read this book. Not because of all the big-ass words, nope! It's because of all the small-ass words we take for granted. It's time to get back into communication.

The definition of "creative" according to our friend the *Merriam-Webster Dictionary* is "having or showing an ability to make new things or think of new ideas." Now you are playing this role as a creative. You are already a creative you see—now it's time to DO something in total IMPROV status to produce. It doesn't matter if you don't know what you are creating yet, it can be as simple as creating new thoughts, new ideas, or new things. If you leave the house in full improv mode, then you will be given inspiration throughout the day. Every hour you remind yourself that YOU are creative and that you are creating beautiful things right now. Does it sound cheesy? Shit, try going to Hollywood—tons of cheesy, well-paid stars there doing this as a job. Well, if you answered yes to this being cheesy, let me tell you what that is. It's your freaking comforting ego, trying to prevent you from doing different things. Wants to make tons of excuses for you so that you don't change. Your ego protects you or so it says. It wants you to do what is normal and conservative and looks good to the other normal, average people of the world. It's protecting your childish spirits from getting laughed at, ignored, and bruised. Too bad you're not a child any longer. In fact, as children, we improvised everything. When we wanted something from our grandparents we played that innocent, sweet, and adorable role. When we wanted mom and dad to buy us that new game? We played a role of loving chores. We adapted and played the part to receive exactly what we wanted, but here you are now—wondering if this will work. First, ask yourself what do you want?

On February 14th, 2016, I walked out of that seminar and never looked back. On the drive home, I knew I needed to start a serious improv role. I immediately became the role of a producer. I looked around in my thoughts and asked, "Who do I want to become that I know now is a producer?" I chose Grant Cardone, best-selling author and international speaker. It's not because I wanted to be Grant Cardone. He is him, and I am me. I wanted to produce like he did, which required tons of energy and action. I began right away acting as if I was already the greatest producer in the world. Try this today, and close the book after this chapter and return to it tomorrow or whenever you're ready. Again, this is not a race. You are beginning a beautiful Comfort Killing journey; there's no one else on your path or in your way.

Choose a quality from the list above and be it. Don't do it—just Be it. To Be something, you must affirm it, believe it, and proclaim it already true. It is your postulate now. Just do that today. Choose a quality and Be that quality or characteristic. Trust me, it gets easier. Here's a quick story of this theory in beingness. Soon after I quit gambling, the feeling of withdrawal was overcoming me and I knew I had to do something about it. The first 30 days were incredibly painful. My ego didn't want to change and learn new patterns. I heard something tell me: "It's okay Stacy, a quick visit to the casino won't hurt." I was battling my own self every minute of the day. I thought about the slots, dreamt about the big win, and even felt like a winner on some days. It appeared as if everything was working for me to go back and gamble. This was the behavior and characteristic I was working to get rid of, day in and day out. But let's take a closer look at what was happening. I had the energy to go if I wanted to. I was clever and creative enough to find money to gamble if I needed it. I was thinking great things to myself that would pump me up and allow me to take massive action towards the casino floor. It was almost effortless how this destructive behavior was working to help me.

I knew that, of course, it was no longer what I wanted —it was hurting me and stunting my growth. It wasn't helping me at all. This is what I did. Every day I would be a non-gambler. I would wait for one of those negative, comforting, and automatic thoughts to come up: "Why not try, Stacy—it's okay" then I would, at that moment, cut the thought short and say to myself, "A non-gambler doesn't think those thoughts." I mean, every single time a thought came to destroy me, I would consciously destroy it. This carried on for months until the negative thoughts stopped coming. It was as if it knew that showing up in my consciousness was no longer worth it. I was Being a non-gambler and taking non-gambling actions for the purpose of having a non-gambler self at the end of it all. It is a cycle, one that requires some work and determination. One that puts you in control of everything in your world. This is how you Be. You keep proclaiming it. Keep postulating it. Choose a quality from the list above or one of your own, and now let's go get a role model or an avatar to help you speed up this behavior change quicker than you once imagined.

Role Models and Persons of Interest

As a Comfort Killer, you will understand the benefits of finding a role model and adapting a few behaviors from him or her for your toolbox. Within your toolbox you should have enough resources to help you through your journey. Now, choosing a role model is important, but it is also vital to know that you cannot be this person in their entirety. You are only clothing yourself with characteristics, qualities, and behaviors that you find attractive. When people want to be like the great Michael Jordan, they are assuming his work ethic, ambition, and his striving for continuous development. This is regardless of their height, skill level, and knowledge of the game. People are just fascinated with his achievements and want to learn what he learned and take the time to train just as hard as he did. Do not become disappointed when you look in the mirror at the end of your role model selection and do not find Mr. Micheal Jordan himself staring back at you. That would only mean that you are inferior and do not understand the mechanism of this principle. Role models help you become the best version of yourself, not the best version of themselves. As I mentioned before, Grant Cardone was my role model selection. I consumed everything he produced, watched videos, read his books, listened to his interviews—I took roughly 5 qualities that inspired me and adopted them. This natural attraction made it easier for me to clothe myself in new habits and behaviors. Here is what I found worked best.

An inferiority complex is something that can ultimately kill us dead. This is because we are living up to the standards and ideas of someone else. We never feel adequate enough in our own skin to perform, and this feeling of being less than—no matter what success we achieve—brings us into apathy, where no action and creativity lives. Just sorry excuses after sorry excuses.

Your role model can be your father, your mother, some actor or philanthropist, entrepreneur, a world changer like Elon Musk ... anyone that truly motivates and inspires your work. Someone might have just popped up in your head just as you were reading this. Who is this person? What have they done that inspires you to action? What makes this person admirable? A hint here is to go totally left. Find someone that will move you outside of your comfort zone completely. Some powerful role models are dead—it's okay to choose dead ones as well; just remember before you choose, think, what qualities do I want to possess? Some dead men and women lived in another time period: The environment was different. Conventional wisdom of that time was different from today, yet their qualities, abilities, unconventional ways of thinking, and strong characteristics may still help you develop even quicker than you thought possible before.

That is why you should really think about who you want to become. This person will only provide you bits and pieces and give you a framework on how to get there, but they will not unlock everything for you. That's why this book is the precursor to your journey, sharing with you the tools that you already have to change your life.

EXERCISE:

First: Write down what you want to change about yourself (personality or habits). This should not be anything material (get a new house, a new car, etc.). This is all about internal qualities.

My example: I hated that I was a procrastinator. I wanted to change my negative thinking. I wanted to get better at making decisions.

Second: Make a list of what you would like to achieve. What person would you like to become, to be known as?

Third: Get confident in who you are and your ability to change your life. Look at your list. Understand that everything you want is already inside of you. You just must dilute the garbage and fill the space with this new identity.

Fourth: Identify a person who displays the characteristics or lifestyle you want. Who inspires you? Who motivates you? Take some time to think about this person and why they appeal to you.

** A role model can be anyone, living or dead, famous or not.

** A role model is someone with a sense of purpose; they are driven and know who *they* are.

Fifth: Choose someone that makes you feel good.

You should always feel good about this process of selecting a role model; you shouldn't feel scared, intimidated, or inferior in any way. If you are, you are selecting the person for the wrong reasons, or you are not selecting the right person. Go back and look at the qualities that you want to adopt and clothe yourself in. Go back and take notes on qualities that you love. Do not be afraid to sit with this process until you are sure that you are moving forward with the person you selected because this is who you are going to be spending time with over the course of 3–6 months. You will be a thief for inspiration, stealing motivation and energy at every chance you get. You will be draining out the bad behavior, bad data, and dumb data and filling yourself with information that suits your beingness.

Not sure if you've picked up on this yet, but you control everything in your life. From the moment you wake up, everything is under your control. It's your universe. You already placed everything there that suits your thinking and actions. You will learn more about this in our mindset filtration chapter. You can change your environment easily. You just must Be first. That is the first step to many processes you will learn in this book.

Before we move on: I would love to know who you are. Take the time and tweet me using the hashtag below.

@StacyACross #TheComfortKillersBook

I am always curious to know how you are doing on your journey to success, and I want you to know that you are supported throughout. At any given time, you can join The Comfort Killers Academy to continue learning and growing.

Visit: www.thecomfortkillers.com

Steal What Works

"Good artists copy; great artists steal."
~ Picasso and Steve Jobs

While you are reading this book, there is no doubt you will leave your comfort zone. I am going to be politically, traditionally, and conventionally incorrect most of the time. I don't care about being normal, especially when my goal is to help millions get uncomfortable to think, act, and live better. It is a crime against humanity to have the need to fit into the status quo—the status quo got you here, *The Comfort Killers* will set you free. You are in a game, whether you believe it or not. Some of you are in the 9–5 game, punch the clock at 6 o'clock game. Being told what to do, and how to do it game. You are in the fear game, unable to speak up because you're terrified you will not be liked game. How about the retirement at 65 game, the unable to enjoy life now game? It is in these games that we end up losing before we get a chance to roll the dice. We all know about the system or the government or the educational game—they are built in society and help to keep us civilized and robotic. No one dares step outside of these prisons we created because we are too afraid of being abnormal. Learn the power within and break the shackles that drag us backwards to death. The bottom line is we are all playing these games or have played them at least once in our lives. That's fine. I create my universe. I understand what I placed on myself for years and lifetimes. I understand at one time it made me feel safe and secure, the need for it then was vital but not anymore. I am breaking the illusions daily, one by one.

The only way to win at the boring game we created for ourselves is to create new ones, so that we have something new to look toward, something we control. To do this we steal what works! There are people living life on their own terms, you might have selected one in the role model process. But these individuals seem to produce like hell, have legacies, change the world, enjoy travel, have great social lives, have great families, make great contributions to society. I always asked myself, "What game are they playing?"

There is a lot of resistance right now inhibiting your next move to freedom. It's there because if too many found out and left this boring game—then who would be left to play it? Who would be left to follow the rules of man when they can be guided by the universe? Who would be left to pay taxes? Who would be left to vote? Everyone can't move to the other side; the world would crumble. That would be the end of this game on earth as we know it. But the good news is there are people like you and I that are enlightened by our inner strength and power, and we are not satisfied. We want to see the world in a brighter ray, and we want to help others do the same. The power that we have within has been withheld through years of inaction. I mean thousands of lifetimes we have been tricked to play a game we did not create, without the tools and know-how to create one that works for us. What is this game we want to create? Well, it's the game of time. To have more time for ourselves and family, more time to love and enjoy the experiences on earth. Don't you want more time to enjoy life and live life to the fullest? Or would you rather be in the rat race heading nowhere fast? Before you know it, you're dead and nobody is at your funeral because there are no memories built up with anyone other than your co-workers. You've invested all your Time on earth in someone else's game. You didn't have the time to create your own. It's easy to blame the government, your parents, tradition, and your lack of knowledge. But at any given point, you might come across good data and feel it. That will be the perfect time to change everything.

I was 34 years old when I created The Comfort Killers to overcome gambling. I didn't sit there and cry about how late in life it finally hit me. I just knew it was time to Be. I couldn't sit around blaming anyone or anything from that point on. Since I was on superhuman mode because I had wasted so much time, I wanted to jump on my journey with tools that I stole from the other game. There's no shame in preparing yourself for the next 5 years of your life. You know what works, right? Steal it!

The first piece of data I stole was Benjamin Franklin's day planner. I first asked myself, how did this individual end up on the 100-dollar bill without being a president? How did this individual invent so many things, and why is he revered as one of the most influential people during his time—and still, to this day? How did he perform, and what actions did he take? After moving to Philadelphia, the attraction to what he has contributed became more real. Above is his daily schedule.

The morning question, What good shall I do this day?	5	Rise, wash, and address *Powerful Goodness*; contrive day's business and take the resolution of the day; prosecute the present study; and breakfast.
	6	
	7	
	8	
	9	Work.
	10	
	11	
	12	Read or overlook my accounts, and dine.
	1	
	2	
	3	Work.
	4	
	5	
	6	Put things in their places, supper, music, or diversion, or conversation; examination of the day.
	7	
	8	
	9	
Evening question, What good have I done today?	10	
	11	
	12	
	1	Sleep.
	2	
	3	
	4	

I was amazed to see how people coordinated and con-structed their lives. It was something I never did before. The first thing I did was steal this structure, implement it, and make it mine. The next thing I stole was understand-ing how money worked. I picked up books on the laws of money and studied it to great lengths. This also helped me know how much of a loser I was, wasting my time (the most valuable asset) and my money in a smoggy and casino daily. I stole the advice of people who had lots and lots of money and began to implement a weekly ritual even when I didn't have any money. I acted as if I did. Weekly, I would sit down and look over my accounts. I was in debt, so this was easy. Then I learned about OPM (other people's money) and how to utilize credit for in-vestments. One by one, doors began opening for me in the form of opportunities.

Don't feel bad when I say to steal anything you can that will help you on this journey. Everything you need is already here in your universe; it all derives from within, the power to observe, assess, and steal! Below are points of interest that you should steal, make your own, and add to your toolbox.

- Foods that provide power and energy
- Tax loopholes
- Creating a LLC for tax benefits and write-offs
- Clinging on to someone who has more, knows more, and does more than you
- Cutting off everything that no longer serves you on this journey (cable TV, friends, parties, any-thing that wastes time)

Remember, you are in a game. The difference is now, you are aware of the game and can create small games within it that you can actually win. A game that you can create very quickly is starting a business. This game alone will help you move out of the larger game. It will provide you more time later, expand your knowledge, and help you to contribute something positive in society.

Other games include:

Live longer to ensure a legacy (quit smoking, eat healthier, create a fitness regimen)

Increase income to remove slave status by creditors (invest in real estate, create or sell something, move on up in your 9 to 5)

Stop negative inputs to focus attention on new ideas

Take time back and use time to create

Not sure about you, but I wasn't taught any of this stuff growing up. I was outside playing in dirt and getting in trouble waiting for another school year to start. My parents didn't know much about this either. My teachers couldn't teach me this.

I went to nursing school a few years after unsuccessfully dabbling in 'finding myself' after high school. The women in my family were of nursing and healthcare backgrounds. They wanted me to do the same. It was a rite of passage. I hated it. I didn't entirely hate it; it just wasn't what I wanted to do. But since I didn't have another solution outside of the game, I played the do-what-makes-others-happy game and enrolled in an expensive endeavor that I would not complete. I remember paying for one clinical class in cash and having the registrar / billing lady look at me like I was crazy for carrying $6,000 in cash and counting it on her desk. She was right in thinking I was crazy. I was. I was crazy for sticking with something I did not enjoy or feel good about. Looking back now, I knew no better and needed that lesson—time, energy, and effort wasted doing something for someone else.

Don't do it for anyone else. Do it because you are doing it for you. Be it because you are being it for you. Have it because you are having it for you. The most important person in this world is you, and without your own happiness, you will be unable to make others happy or contribute anything good. Be careful when choosing your games. Know that you are 100% feeling it.

In Jack Canfield's book *The Success Principles*, I learned of a guidance system that we are all born with. It tells us when we are on or off purpose by the amount of joy we are receiving at any given moment. Throughout this book, I tend to reference feeling a lot. This is because I believe in feelings; I believe that joy is the most important gift we receive in our human lives. When we are happy we are on purpose. We will talk more about goals and purpose later in this book. For now, know that it is okay to steal anything you want. Again, it is your universe. You put everything in it, things that will hurt you and steer you down a destructive path, as well as tools that will help you get back on your journey to success again. Do not be afraid to steal it. It's already yours.

CHANGE THE MINDSET

Your mindset is comprised of the sum of your thoughts, habits, behaviors, beliefs, and subconscious. It's the first thing that must be changed when you are taking a new forward, more-positive step in life. Once you change your mindset, it's hard to see and think how you once did. This will help you reshape your universe, create your game, and WIN at anything you set out to do. Point blank. The one thing that has gotten in your way is your mindset. I've written many articles on this subject because I believe it requires continuous attention. The mind is such a beauty when it is positive but such a freaking enemy when it is negative and destructive.

At the first moment of returning home from the free seminar I walked out of on February 14, 2016, I pulled out my journal and began to write. I wrote down the craziest, most unattainable, and most unreasonable goals I could think of. I wrote, I AM AN AUTHOR, I EARN MILLIONS OF DOLLARS IN BUSINESS, I AM A SPEAKER ....

I wrote until it filled up 3 pages of my journal. I wasn't scared anymore. My mindset would have to catch up to me because I was unstoppable. If you stop and think HOW, you've already lost. The moment you question your Beingness with the word HOW, your square peg returns to square one. It doesn't matter how! It only matters that you believe it. You Be-lieve it! The difference between my mindset February 14, 2016, and today is that it has expanded into accepting my beliefs. That is all. Before, I would talk myself out of such beliefs by saying, "I don't have the money" or "I don't have the knowledge or expertise" or "I don't know the right people." None of these were true—it was self-doubt and fear imposed upon me through my limited mindset and beliefs. Mindset is everything—it must be the next area to tackle on your journey to success. Think of it this way. Your mindset is a magnet with the power to attract to it anything it wants. If it is negative, it attracts negativity in the form of bad breaks, horrific breakups, traffic, arguments, no job opportunities, no growth opportunities, fights, struggles, increasing debt, low-energy people and situations, or bad karma. If it is positive and expansive, it will attract people, things, and places that are positive and expansive. It really is as simple as that concept.

Your mind is not who you really are. You have been on automatic mode up until this point. No fault of yours— you didn't know. But now you know, and once you know, you must do something about it. You are ignorant without data. I am giving you the data. I've tested this data and used it to level up in my personal and business lives. So how do you change your mindset? Well, here's what I did.

Warning: This takes work and practice. If you complete this game for 7 days, you will have opened your mind up more than you have done in 7 years.

NONCAT EXERCISE [NOT ONE NEGATIVE, COMMENT, ACTION, OR THOUGHT]

Step 1: Say to yourself that you demand your mind to expand positively.

Step 2: Practice NONCAT for 24 hours.

Step 3: Journal your results.

Example:

> Hour 1: Had a negative thought about my boss at work
>
> Hour 5: Negative action: gossiping at work

The moment you have a negative comment, action, or thought—START OVER.

Do this until you can successfully complete 24 hours of pure positivity. Here is what will happen. You will start to notice that you have major control over your mind, actions, words, and thoughts. You've always had this control—but you gave up control to suit the norm and the average. Today you take it back.

You will also notice pure beauty in having control over NONCAT. You will start to look for something positive to say as a redirection of that negative thing. You will be floating through time and space, owning your thoughts and controlling your behavior. You are now training your mind. This takes practice, and I advise that you do not move ahead in this book before completing a successful day. It may take you 2 months. Who cares. It is not a race. You are no longer in competition with the world. You are dominating your journey to success.

Before we move on, take the time to add me on all your socials and then say hello!

Twitter – @stacyacross

Instagram – @stacyacross

It took me some time to take back control over my thoughts during my journey. That's how I know it's a critical step. I am still cleaning out the mess that I created. It's a daily habit, and you have got to help yourself to succeed at this process.

You might want to add a notification to your mobile's calendar. Every few hours, have it pop up with: What Are You Thinking? Is it Positive? Get Back on Track. Make a calendar reminder for 2–3 months from now and tell your future self to remain uncomfortable and get on task. These are things that you have got to get used to doing because no one else will do them for you. We are habit-forming, clothes-wearing creatures. Start forcing the issue. I understand everything's not as peachy as other writers claim they are. They leave information out of their books so that you are at a never-ending search of the Truth. My intentions are to give you everything here, all in one place, usable data that you can utilize to work out all your previous issues. Then you get to a place of change, but your old mindset doesn't even know how to recognize change.

I listened to a random podcast one day featuring some guy that was in prison and was given a second chance at life upon his release. Throughout the podcast he kept saying to the host, I tried everything until something stuck. He had a ruthless daily schedule to include hours of personal development, fitness, and business training. He did yoga and meditation, and he even added acupuncture. He ran, jogged, and sat in silence. He changed and rearranged his schedule to force change. He used apps for Android. He wrote in journals. He did whatever it took to change. He knew only 1 thing: he wanted to get out of the destructive mindset, the one that most criminals have, the type of mindset that falls back into the comforting arms of the prison system. He wanted out, and he pushed himself to achieve it. I was fascinated with his attempts to change. At the time I was listening to this podcast, I was starting to recognize my own destructive behaviors as well and begging myself for change. In fact, I made an oath to myself that I would listen to podcasts, audiobooks, and positive meditative affirmations only during my commute and while in my car. I completely shut off talk radio, sports radio, and music. I was strictly using my car as a moving university. So, this ex-inmate goes on to say he practiced and practiced and practiced, until out of nowhere, he started to recognize his change. He felt different. He responded differently and was doing things that only forced him to grow. It made me think of change as a doable, actionable thing rather than a destination. In order to do we must Be.

The 3 Cs of CCCHANGE

"Growth and comfort do not co-exist."
~ Ginny Rometty

Motivation is a big word; so is fear, and so is passion. Throughout this book, we define BIG words as words that matter, not words that are long in character that mean nothing to either you or me in terms of personal development.

We learned so many things and never really understand why. What is the reasoning behind certain aspects of life, for example Time? Have you ever looked up the word Time? What is time, and where did it all go?

I can honestly take a guess at how many will actually completely read this book out of 100% ... Some will go create more time after reading this section, and others will abandon this entire thing and call it a fluke because they didn't change a thing. Listen, you have got to stop bitchin' about time. If you have time for TV, football, gossip talk over the phone, Snapchat, Facebook, going out to the movies, dinner, or the bar then you have time for this book.

There are no excuses if you don't want any. Excuses are plentiful when you so much as think of one.

So, don't talk to me about time. Okay, talk to me about time. Let's look it up! Grab your *Merriam-Webster* and write down the definition of time.

Definition: Time

_____

_____

_____

From now on you will begin to find deeper meanings in words. Time for me isn't just the seconds, hours, and minutes represented in a day. That's the literal, reasonable, and surface meaning. I hope you'll begin to take note of the illogical and unreasonable definitions such as:

- a period of apprenticeship
- the point or period when something occurs
- an appointed, fixed, or customary moment or hour for something to happen, begin, or end
- the measured or measurable period during which an action, process, or condition exists or continues
- one of a series of recurring instances or repeated action
- a person's experience during a certain period

What!? I never looked at Time in such a deep way until I started looking words up. During this program, try to pull illogical ways of looking at the meaning of words, because conventional wisdom keeps us out of time. We need to rip to shreds everything we thought we knew about a word because, honestly, you cannot be in communication with the world and yourself if you are running around telling me and everyone else that you have no time, especially if you do not even know what the damn word symbolizes.

Let's get practical then:

How many hours in a day?

_____

How many hours in a week?

_____

How many hours in a month?

_____

How many hours in a year?

_____

All those damn hours, where did they go? Really, where do they go? Did you know the answers, or did you have to multiply like I had to? Isn't it funny that when people say, "Oh I don't have the time," you can ask, "How many hours are in a week?" and they'll get stumped? How the hell can you say you don't have something that you know nothing about? Are you measuring your day? Try asking someone out of the 128 hours they have all week, how much is spent working, exercising, watching TV, eating, sleeping, playing, reading, on social media, cooking, taking the kids to daycare, spending time with family and friends, clubbing, grocery shopping, napping, commuting, meditating, or whatever.

People do not know where they stand. It is an absolute ignorance to spew excuses about Time when they don't know how much of it is there or where its allocated. Please understand this concept. This is awareness—this is how we shift our mindset. Understanding what we speak affects what we receive. This is our first point in basics. #UnLearnEverything

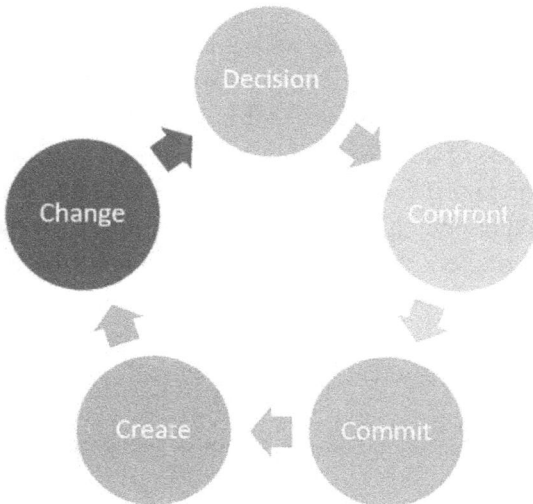

Before we get into the 3 Cs of CCCHANGE, let us briefly talk about the 5 points that need to happen for an awareness shift to occur in a person's life. I am sharing each point because I have gone through them myself. Forget about trying to be a perfectionist, planning and preparing for right now. You will not need to be hell-bent on finding out what your life's purpose is in this step. I only want to develop your mind to think differently.

1.   **DECISION** – You made the decision to purchase, download, steal, or borrow this book, and I commend you either way.

DEFINITION: Decision

_____

_____

_____

_____

Do you have authority over your life? In order to make a decision you must first be presented with a choice, and that choice has power and consequence (or karma). Everything we do and everything we decide to do is followed by specific results or pathways that lead us to another process of deciding.

When you tell yourself that you do not have control, you are experiencing a state of confusion, doubt, by having a slave mentality. The short list below will help you understand how one gives up control of his/her life.

- I was born in a poor family. That is why my life sucks.
- The government doesn't do enough for people like me.
- I can't get a job because no one is hiring right now.

- The economy is bad right now, so I can't start a business.
- I am not smart enough to be a lawyer, doctor, or judge.
- My boss is always holding me back from promotions.
- I am dyslexic; that is why I can't do that job or activity.

That is just to name a few. I could go on.

Automatically, your mind will try to keep you in a slave mentality because it's a culmination of past decisions, tradition, and conventional wisdom. Your *think* is wounded. It was abused for as long as you were alive, and it's about time you change that shit.

Decision means control. Take the control back in your life. In order to change, you must have decided somewhere down the line that you are sick and tired of being sick and tired. You've been living in a matrixed cycle of sleep, work, sleep, tv, sleep, work, kids, family, eat, sleep, work. That is boring as hell!

Think of three decisions you made today or recently when a choice was presented to you. See you have to decide to turn on the TV, you have to decide to sleep all day, you have to decide if you are going to go to the gym or not.

The bigger problem is how automatic it is making bad decisions. Doesn't it suck that you didn't even have a choice in the decision-making process? Your brain is automatically drawn to comfort and slavery. Your subconscious has CONTROL over you. You didn't even think about it … and you chose some low-energy activity. Your *think* is bruised.

Let's take some control back.

Consciously be aware of what you are thinking throughout the day. This is crazy hard to do—not going to lie to you—but if you make it a point to do it, you will start to focus on everything you are thinking. You will be in control of your thoughts.

Even if you catch yourself thinking, making a decision, "talking to yourself," day dreaming, thinking negative thoughts, positive thoughts. I want you to tell yourself THANK YOU FOR MAKING ME AWARE. Jot down your experiences throughout the week. Document your journey.

Make the decision out loud, right now that you will focus your energy on your THINK starting now.

_____

_____

_____

_____

_____

_____

_____

_____

_____

_____

_____

_____

_____

_____

_____

_____

2.   **CONFRONT** – You experienced ups and downs in life; we all go through it. You need to question the very thing that has got you scared, upset, confused, doubtful, energetic, mad, emotional.

DEFINITION: Confront

_____

_____

_____

_____

The secret that everyone whispers to you about is this: You will always be stuck on a particular level if the tests of that level have not been confronted. You must put attention to the very thing that you hate or fear in order to move on.

Let's say you are in debt. You hate seeing piles and piles of collection bills in the mail; you hate when they call your phone and definitely when they call your job. You put everything far away in some corner or desk drawer and never return to it. Years have passed. You've been doing this for quite some time. You complain about being in debt and having no money for the finer things in life. You settle for second best. Your finances are really one part of your life that you'd rather not talk about. A feeling of disgust and fear builds up in your belly. Your electricity gets cut off every other month. You hate paying bills. You argue and fight over money with other people—you borrow more money than you know you can pay back. You begin to steal and lie. You are never honest when you speak about what is going on in your financial life. You try to play the part—try to beat the Smiths. You cannot afford the things you have, but you want them anyway. Your school debt has defaulted. Certified mail is now coming.

Your taxes aren't filed because, you figure, you won't get a return anyway. Three years have passed. You're digging a hole only the lottery can fix. You want quick fixes. You look to the casino, your family, and scratch-offs. You dig deeper until—

You make a decision: "I need to do better with my money."

At any point, one could have made the decision to take back control, and I hope that after reading this book, more people look at control this way. To have control is to make a decision that moves you forward, no matter the circumstance, regardless of socioeconomic impact. By the very act of decision-making, you will inevitably confront one thing or another.

Here is another point to make. You can decide and then do nothing about it. That's not good either. A proper decision is only effective if you confront the very thing in question.

Example: I need to go to the gym.

Decision: I'll go to the gym right now.

Confronting: I am not healthy, and I understand that if I continue to eat unhealthy and not exercise I will ruin my life. How did I get here? What daily decisions do I continue to make that creates this unhealthy lifestyle? Why am I making these decisions?

Example: I am going to focus on my finances.

Decision: I will create a budget today as to create a better financial future in my life.

Confronting: I need to take all my bills out of the closet and see where I stand. What brought me here. What do I have to do to create a better financial future? Who does this affect? Are there any resources that will help me? How much do I make now? Do I need a second job?

When you confront something, you deal with the problem face-to-face and in a direct way. Doing it this way will be painful, but in order to move forward this step cannot be avoided.

"... I started to realize how many great things could happen by confronting the things that scare you most."
~ David Archuleta

3.   **COMMIT** – Great things will happen once you fully commit to a goal, target, or result. The very act of commitment allows the genius from within to pull to it exactly what it desires.

DEFINITION: Commit

_____

_____

_____

_____

A commitment is a promise to yourself, which is connected to substance through accountability. I believe that we should stop lying to ourselves. Think about it this way. Whatever happens when you lie to other people—no matter the size, depth, and scope of that lie—it's unethical. I understand that sometimes we all don't express the total truth. I get it. Someone went a step further by categorizing these little lies. We now know them as white lies. Either way it sucks to be lied to, and it feels even worse when a friend, family member, coworker, coach, teammate, spouse, girlfriend, or boyfriend has you figured for a liar. But what happens when we lie to ourselves? Isn't this 10 times worse? Imagine you promised yourself that you would get up early to begin an exercise regimen in the early mornings. The next morning, you push snooze and later pushed the button again. Next thing you know, you end up snoozing through your planned exercise time and wake up when you normally do. You have just lost faith in yourself. You just confirmed that you were weak and that your promise and commitment means nothing. Who in their right mind will trust you or support you if you cannot keep promises to yourself? You wonder why you are getting the same results—it's because you keep breaking promises to yourself.

In order for true commitment to take place, you need to stop breaking promises to yourself. It's more beneficial that you do not make a promise or commitment if you know you will not succeed 100%. When you achieve this, your subconscious will start etching a new mindset in place. Your subconscious will begin to believe you and then give you the power to take control of your actions. You feel tired because you lie to yourself. You press the snooze button over and over again because you have lied to yourself so many times that it has become effortless to break new commitments.

In this case, in order to reprogram your consciousness at the deepest level, you have to become aware of all the lies you tell yourself. Then thank yourself for becoming more aware of your thoughts and how your actions affect you. Thank your subconscious for taking the time to record all your previous behaviors and broken promises, but allow it to transcribe new behaviors and better promises.

Test yourself. Think:

Today, I will do 100 sit-ups. *Then do them*

Today, I will budget and look over my finances. *Then do it.*

Today, I will eat salad. *Then do it.*

What you are doing is reprogramming commitment to mean follow-through and achievement—not weakness, doubt, and comfort.

Do this from now on. Become conscious of all the small, medium, and large demands and obligations you give yourself and watch how you begin to gain new understanding and appreciation for commitment.

Remember, don't lie to yourself! If you know that you will not complete an action—don't write it down, don't agree to it, don't say it, and don't even think it.

Write three promises that you plan to commit to this week (I already took care of the first one):

1 – I will complete this book in its entirety.

_____

_____

_____

4.   **CREATE** – We were made of the same stuff as the stars. The source being the creator, and you being made within the same spirits means that you have been given an awesome gift, to create. Try it out sometime!

DEFINITION: Create

_____

_____

_____

_____

If you want total change then you have got to get in the habit of creating the person you wish to become. The only way you create this magnificent person is by adding new ideas, new focus, and new inventions.

I am currently in the process of losing weight. This is my goal: Lose Weight + Increase Energy to maintain the high level of activity needed for success.

I need the energy and since I cannot create new energy, I need to increase it. This causes a change in my health, which then changes my body type, which allows me to perform at high levels <u>ALL</u> the time. As a result, a new me is created.

You are given all the necessary resources to create anything you want in this lifetime. Look around you. The chair you are sitting in, somebody created that. The pen you are writing with, someone created that also. The internet was a creation.

Remember, it starts with thought and ends in creation. Words on a paper are a new creation.

5.   **CHANGE** – We should never want to remain the same person year after year. It means that we have not acted towards growth. Do you want more? In order to change, we must want a new direction and more out of life: Health, Wealth, or Happiness, which is CK360—The Entire Scope of Life.

DEFINITION: Change

_____

_____

_____

_____

Goals and Purpose

What is the end result here? What are we changing ourselves to do and achieve? Well that's where goals come in, and to help me help you, I have to give credit where it's due. On my journey, I've built relationships with people that moved me forward. I received clues and bits of information that helped me progress. You will attract these types of people too. It is inevitable to be on such a mission and not receive valuable data over the course of your journey. All you have to be is aware of what is happening and handle it accordingly. Take some, not all. For everything that you hear isn't for you, and surely everything that you see is not all for you to take either. Steal what works and discard what doesn't.

Let's play a game. Answer the questions below:
1. What one thing do you desire to achieve?
2. Why do you desire that one thing?
3. What are you willing to sacrifice or give to obtain that one thing?
4. When do you want that one thing?
5. When are you willing to start?

Take some time and deeply think about the answers to the questions above. This will help with your goal-setting framework. Goals are long-term and related to an activity that is measured in years or more. They are known objectives toward which your actions and activities are directed with the purpose of achieving it. Goals are to be written in an achieved or an accomplished state.

Example: I am the bestselling author of 5 books or I earn $83,333 per month in my business.

Writing them in an achieved state will allow you to focus on Being. You are doing only to catch up to the state you are already are in. Plus, writing it in such a form helps us to align all the needed energy and activities in the right frame and perspective. The perspective is in a first-person state—from cause, not effect. When you are at cause, you control it all. You control your input, throughput, and output. Your purpose should ask the question, "What do I have to do to get to the goal—to be at cause?"

The goal extraction framework above has a "no how" approach. The how doesn't matter. Most people get confused with purpose and goals and how to set them. I was also at one time at a loss of what I truly wanted out of life. Some folks have 10 goals that they are always writing down. I only want a big one that will cover the basis of all my goals. For example, my goal is:

I influence millions of people through my voice and energy in speaking and writing. I help millions of people get uncomfortable to think better, act better, and live better.

I understood early on that the more I help and the more I give, the more I receive. The more energy that I produce and give, the more it comes back to me in the form of support, money, and opportunities. There is no limit to how much I will receive.

I used to write every day that I earn $83,000 per month. Then I realized that was way too small. I used to write that I coach 5 people per month @ a rate of $2500 per person. Then I realized that was way too small.

So why not have a BIG goal that I work towards on purpose that can cover all my bases. If I am influencing millions of people (which now that I think about it, is too few) then surely, I will be earning way more than $83,000 per month and coaching way more than 5 people per month. I would be on my way to freedom and contributing to a better society. Find something that holds no weight to expansion, that does not have an anchor or limit, and then work towards that. Leave the small goals to those unwilling to get uncomfortable.

If I influenced millions that would mean I am an excellent communicator, writer, speaker, and motivator! It all boils down to the balloon you have floating on top of your head, and the purpose is to get your head wrapped around that huge balloon through activity and action!

Give Yourself Permission

A friend of mine living in Australia once said to me, "Well, how much do YOU want, Stacy?" after I asked him how much I should sell one of my webinars for. I didn't understand his answer. I couldn't wrap my head around charging more than $49.00 for my time, effort, and energy. My mindset hadn't expanded that much yet, and I was left guessing and doubting my value.

Fast forward to the present. I charge for the energy I put into the universe. Your time is very valuable, and the faster you know and understand this concept the faster you stop wasting it and start getting energy back for it. In the beginning when working through my self-improvement, I never quite gave myself permission. I was my worst enemy, saying things such as, "I am not an expert. I am not good enough. No one will listen to me." You sort of get slammed when people don't respond to your material the way you imagined. That's fine. You still have got to give yourself permission to succeed. I only can think of Jesus walking around Jerusalem, speaking this new approach to living, thinking, and being. The majority of people did not listen. They condemned him, they spit at him, and disregarded his wisdom. He never gave up during his travels—from 1 person to the next he gave himself permission. He knew that his beliefs were God-sent, and he needed to complete his mission, his goal, and his purpose. No matter what. No excuses and by any means necessary. Thousands of years later, we are still singing his praise and speaking his name.

Why is it hard for us, then, to give ourselves permission? It may not be your fault. Again, our subconscious can either work for us or against us, and mine was totally working against me. I couldn't even see past the negatives I told myself about why I couldn't achieve something.

The Subconscious Mind:

What is the subconscious mind? It is not easily accessible to you in your waking consciousness. Your subconscious stores data, visual images, habits, skills, experiences, and thoughts that you have accumulated throughout your entire life and past lives. It stores beautiful and wonderful experiences as well as the painful, traumatic, and sad ones. In contrast, your conscious mind observes, assesses, generates thoughts, and applies logic to your experiences. Your consciousness is 100% under your control, but your subconscious mind is functioning automatically without your control. Your subconscious controls your heartbeat and your blood circulation, and it stores DNA data. Your conscious mind gives direct orders to the subconscious mind and is able to make decisions. Depending on the programming of your subconscious mind, it will either accept the direction or request given by your conscious mind or it will reject it. The subconscious mind is so powerful that it can override your conscious mind and carry out instructions without effort or questioning. Ingrained in your subconscious you have all your daily habits, behaviors, and beliefs, even limited beliefs (I can't do such and such, I am not an expert, I can't charge this much, I am not good enough … etc.) stored and taking over your consciousness. Here is a scary stat according to *Psychology Today* if you are ready for it; 88% of your mind is made up of your subconsciousness, while only 12% is under your conscious control. Knowing this data, the next question should be "F#*K, how can I reprogram it!?"

First, you should ask yourself if your sub-mind is programmed to help you succeed or support your failure.

There are a few ways to reprogram your subconscious, but just like our NONCAT exercise, it is going to require practice, practice, and more practice. If you are ready then carry on!

I must warn you again—it's going to take practice. You cannot just put up a Facebook ad and leave the thing running without checking the stats and giving yourself time to test and retest. You are so important that you should be showering yourself with time to develop and grow. This is a HUGE step in your journey, as no one will be able to do it for you.

At one point in my life, I moved to Delaware. At this point, I was still heavily addicted to gambling. I would dodge eviction notices on my door by taking out payday loans. I would lie to my partner about my habits. I wanted to change that side of my life so bad but didn't know how. I didn't know how to change my current habits because they felt so automatic, so natural and effortless. If I had any spare dollars, and sometimes not-so-spare dollars, like clockwork I would take off to the casino. I was mad at myself every time I left the place. I was losing so much of my money and my confidence there; I felt like I didn't know which way to turn. I felt hopeless, helpless, and sorry for myself. I was in a state of self-pity, which is a horrible place be. I couldn't look anyone in the eye, because I wasn't really there. My mind was only focused on when and how the hell could I get back in the casino. At family gatherings, I wasn't there. I was missing out birthdays, weddings, and special occasions with friends and family. Most of the time it was because I couldn't afford to go. The reason I couldn't afford to go was because every dollar was spent in the casino. There were times when I chose to go gamble with my last $20.00 instead of buying food. This was how crazy and dire my situation was. It had gotten so bad that I would do ANYTHING to change, but for God's sake I would NOT be going to a Gambler's Anonymous meeting. It was due to the fear of telling others that I had a problem. My partner found out, and she started keeping a close eye on our finances. My game was being exposed, and little by little, another lie was given as a cover-up. The problem still persisted. It was now an automatic behavior. After nine years of a serious gambling addiction, one would think I needed drastic measures like a hypnosis session or a swift kick in the head. I definitely needed the latter after watching ALL my money—and money that I didn't have—go down the drain.

I started to take small actions on helping me change. Four tools helped me overcome and redirect my gambling addiction. These same tools can help you overcome any negative programming you have currently ingrained in your subconscious. I must forewarn you again—it takes practice, but it works magic!

Visualization:

This method is standalone the best thing you can do to help reprogram your subconscious. The truth of the matter is that your subconscious does not know what is real and what is made up or imagined. It stores everything as experienced and real. The beautiful part about your consciousness is that you can trick your subconscious into reprogramming new scenes and imaginings that are manufactured to help you succeed. I used to visualize days without going to the casino. I would literally make up scenes in my mind's eye—of me going to the gym, making breakfast, smiling, being happy, seeing family, spending time with my partner, and living my life. I imagined me driving past the casino and not even thinking twice about it. I imagined me loving life again.

I am not even going to lie—it was tough. I would go to the casino at times after visualizing, and in the back of my head was this pounding truth that would make me feel bad and scared to be there. It was me telling myself that this was wrong. It no longer matched my lifestyle. It started getting HARDER to go to the casino than it used to. I still was addicted, but I definitely was consciously thinking of how it made me feel, how bad I wanted to stop, how it was ruining my life. These thoughts were non-existent at one point. Before that I would just go, lose my money, get mad, and lie to my partner. No hard feelings. I didn't have a care.

I remember one day after continuously using these tools to reprogram, I heard something during a gym session that to this day gives me the chills. I was listening to some 50 Cent mixtape while walking on the treadmill, totally disengaged from both the walk and the song that was playing. All of a sudden, in my headset, I heard very clearly, "You have a gambling problem!" I immediately got goose bumps all over my body and jumped the hell off the treadmill. I stopped the song and stood there in disbelief and horror of what I just heard. I looked around – everyone's life was normal as they didn't quite understand what the hell just happened to me. I was afraid to rewind the song because I knew it wasn't the song. It was my subconscious. That was the first of many awakenings that I would have while living in Delaware during my addiction. It all started to flurry in and through me during the reprogramming phase of my journey.

To visualize: Give yourself 30 minutes to an hour of quiet time and close your eyes. Lay down or sit up straight. Begin to visually imagine in your mind's eye your ideal scene. What are you wearing? What are you driving? Where do you live? How are you dressed? What are you saying? Imagine with the colors, sounds, and smells of the scenes. It is very important to lock the entire scene in.

Again, your subconscious will accept anything you give it as truth and fact—that it has already happened. It will begin to use the new scenes (if you give it enough) to help guide you to success. It will remember when you felt good during a speaking engagement and provide it back to you. **[Repeat Daily.]**

Steve Jobs used visualization to vividly imagine the iPhone and its functionality before it was ever designed or built.

Affirmations:

Affirmations are vital. The definition of an affirmation is a proclamation, an agreement. This technique has helped me so much that I was able to create my own set of affirmations for The Comfort Killers. Since every belief and habit you already have is formed by repetition, you can use the same process to reprogram your subconscious but this time with success in mind. You've written down some qualities in a previous chapter. Qualities that your role model possesses. Well, now it's time to BE! Our goal with affirmations is to develop new habits by planting positive messages in your subconscious. We have limited beliefs, and they usually start with these two words: I can't. These negative feelings and actions materialize in the form of lack and failure in your outward universe. Someone probably told you that you "couldn't," or you've probably seen your mother say she "can't" or you "can't" and you "won't," and now it is a belief deep inside you. It's time to change that. Repetition of an affirmation can "rewire the patterns in our brain with cognitive behavioral therapy or affirmations. Affirmations change the way our brains are wired and the brain lights up differently" says practicing neuropsychiatrist Dr. Mona Lisa Schulz, MD, Ph.D.

I love telling the story of how I introduced affirmations in my life. I was in such a need of a mental switch that I had to go AWOL with them. I printed out tons and tons of affirmations and hung them up all over my apartment in Delaware. The bathroom, kitchen, walls, mirrors, doors—just everywhere. I tricked myself. Just when I thought it was safe! Boom! Another affirmation in my face. I had an app on my phone, I had notecards—I was constantly feeding my brain new beliefs and positive information to store. Things started changing. You will notice awesome changes too—just keep doing it.

Examples of Affirmations
1. I am strong and powerful
2. Others look up to me as a leader because of my confidence
3. My beliefs manifest my reality
4. I attract success into my life
5. I have the power to manifest my dreams
6. I always find a way to make money
7. I am attracting money and growing my bank
8. Money is everywhere
9. I am at peace with my guilt
10. I am a highly motivated person

You will start to notice how these affirmations become your new thoughts! Take some time to compile affirmations, print them out, and load them on your phone. Do whatever it takes to reprogram!

Meditation:

Comfort Killers, let me just drop a plug right here and now for this tool that was given to us by the universe! It has been instrumental in my growth. Now before I get into the positive effects of meditation and why it WILL reprogram your subconscious in a powerful way, let me share a quick story about what happened to me during a meditation session.

Now, I didn't know what the heck I was doing. Again, everything I was trying was because I wanted to QUIT gambling. I needed to. It was ruining my life and changing the person I thought I was. I got into meditation because I heard that it worked. No one sat and told me how to meditate though, and I thought I was doing it wrong every time, until I realized that the act of learning how to meditate is a discipline that one must go through as a novice. I wasn't the Buddha or anything. I just lay there and closed my eyes and breathed. To completely stop thinking was the hardest thing in the world. Complete silence and no thoughts? Yeah, right! After some practice and guided meditation videos on YouTube, I started getting a little better. I would literally meditate daily, sometimes for 20 minutes, other times for 2 hours. Before bed, I would put on my headphones and just fall asleep to an 8 hour long binaural meditation mp3. This was how bad I wanted it. I needed to feel the change. It wasn't much longer until I got better at slipping into the meditation, clearing my chakras, and allowing light to consume me. Each time after my meditation session, I would feel light and full of energy. Back in Delaware again, another awakening took place, and this time it scared the living daylights out of me. More about my experience in a later chapter.

Meditation is a beautiful journey people take with themselves to quiet the noise and get true support from their higher self. This creative source self provides intuitions, visions, and anything else you ask of it.

To meditate: Start off with digestible time periods to meditate. Give yourself 15 minutes to 45 minutes to begin with if you have never meditated before. If you have meditated before and understand the concepts, just repeat this daily as meditation does wonders to reprogram the subconscious mind. When your mind is still, relaxed, and silenced—it is highly programmable. You may plant anything you want in that space. Whether you want to know more about who you are and enhance it or drop bits and pieces of data to create the reality you want. Meditation helps you focus, concentrate, and remove distraction both in meditation and out.

Everyone's result in meditation will be different. My experience is mine and only for me. You will have other experiences. It is always a good idea to write down how you feel and what you see during your meditation, once you are finished.

Positive Self Talk:

I talk to myself more than anyone will ever talk with me. I am always with myself, and I have a relationship with myself. What we say during these talks through thought or voice is extremely telling of what is going on subconsciously. Your talk is a powerful affirmation within itself. It pains me to hear people say negative things to themselves such as "Bad things always happens to me," "I always fail," or "Nothing ever works out." Sometimes they say things like, "I'll never find a job" or "I can't afford that dress." All these are reprogrammable if only you are conscious to begin with. Remember, your conscious mind uses logic, assesses risk, thinks up thoughts, and does all the beautiful thing it's designed to do while we are awake. But, what you say, your subconscious believes. That is why it's easy for one to say these negative things, while others trained themselves to only say positive things and positivity is easier for them. Your self-talk has got to be positive because it is directly related to your attitude and emotion as well. You are given a choice. All humans have free choice, and we are able to respond to anything that happens in our life or take the lower avenue and react to anything that happens as a result.

Try using only positive words to describe your feelings. If someone asks, "How is your day," you tell them "Fantastic! I feel great!" even when you may have a headache or are feeling a little tired. It takes real guts to say something positive in a negative situation, and it takes real guts to continue to do it in all areas of your life! I am glad you have guts, my friend; you are a Comfort Killer!

Everything is Within Reach

I was sitting in my dining room with an internet connection the next morning after my life started over. It was February 15, 2016. I had walked out from a seminar with my energy on peak and my mind in motion. I don't know where I would start. I am not sure how to really begin. Many of you will be in this exact position of not knowing but know enough to know that you gotta move. There I was listening to my role model again, Grant Cardone. I decided that I would create a website and get involved in personal development and self-improvement. I typed in the search bar: Comfort Killers. Thousands of results came back, but they weren't what I was expecting.

"Motives of a Serial Killer."

I am happy to announce right here in this book that I successfully removed serial killer websites from the #1–#7 spot on Google. That was my goal when I typed in this new name for my company that I had no idea I was making.

Comfort Killers are serial killers? Not on my watch!

I didn't ask how. I just started typing.

www.thecomfortkillers.com | Domain

Goal – A place to house all my articles, podcasts, webinars, etc., etc. I knew nothing about marketing. All my previous businesses didn't even have LLCs. I was brand new to this world of entrepreneurship, because this time it felt real. I switched focus for my podcast show: "Get Uncomfortable with Stacy A. Cross" to celebrate my newfound love of self-improvement and deleted ALL my older episodes—the ones that did NOT align to my new mission. For I was still a gambler in them. I was still someone that I didn't want to showcase. I was not myself. I deleted, edited, and started over. I didn't see an end. I didn't even know that it was the beginning.

Many times, you're going to get to a time when everything starts at zero and everything is easier to maneuver and handle. You're going to know this time because your brain is a blank canvas and you want to do it all to show yourself that you can. For two months, I kept pounding at it, writing, blogging, adding, and increasing my results. Nothing could stop me. I was everywhere online. I wanted to make a grand entry. People started to take notice and supported this mission that I was on. It was not even clear yet, but it was definitely something that caught people's attention. They were super happy that a fresh voice with a story and a website was coming into a space that was already crowded. They wanted someone new. This person would be me. I started to get random emails from people wanting to support the company, and myself. They wanted to help take it off the ground. That's how I met my first investor and business partner, James Flanagan.

I wanted to say this. You may not know right now where you will end up, but you have got to keep going. If you can see it, you can reach it. If you can visualize it, you can reach it. If you can speak it, you can certainly reach it. Even when things may not look pretty—keep going. Keep putting your energy out there and into your work and you will attract the right people at the right time that are WILLING to help you with no strings. Whether you are starting a side hustle, a side job, or a siding company— keep going. Do something for it daily. Don't skip a day. People will take notice; you have just become attractive.

Let's talk about the law of attraction for a moment.

> You are changing your mindset (check)
> You are working on your goals (check)
> You want to start a business (check)
> You have selected a role model (check)
> You are clothing yourself with new behaviors, thoughts, and attitude (check)
> *You are becoming super attractive to those who*

Have changed their mindset (check)
Have goals to help individuals working toward
their goals (check)
Have started a business and now is giving back,
ready for mentorship, etc. (check)
Respond well to people with positive mindsets,
attitudes, and behaviors (check)

The law of attraction is working all the time; it's a
law. It's just like gravity, constantly working on mass and
matter. You don't have to see it to believe it, you just know
and understand the concept because you cannot disprove
it. You throw something up in the air … it's going to come
right down. Natural and supernatural at the same time.
Just as the forces of gravity is working regardless of your
adherence, the law of attraction is doing its thing. My
worst fears are being attracted to me. Your thoughts are
vibrational, which send off magnetic waves (thought
particles) to the very thing you want. The problem is, we
can't remain positive, abundance, or faithful to that one
thing. Problems get in our way, and we start sending
mixed signals into the universe. Some people whose
thoughts are pure and clear of doubt receive almost instant
materialization. Their thoughts are realized at a much
quicker rate than others. When we believe we know and
we believe it to be true, the universe adopts the reality we
are constantly visualizing and realizing is true. Let's say
the average person's vibrational waves oscillate at a rate of
20,000, a number we can just use as a benchmark to gauge.
Then what about the person who is continually improving
his mind, body and spiritual awareness, he may be oscillating at 25,000? A person who has achieved great clarity and
who is in flow maybe oscillating at 50,000. That's when
you are no longer bogged down by society's norms. You
are living on your own terms and totally aware and conscious

of the world within you and without you. You are just creating left and right with no effort. A floating body with unconditional love for all and through all. That person's energy is so attractive that thoughts become materialized at a faster rate. This person has got to watch what he thinks up and guard their energy like Fort Knox.

I've felt a glimpse of this when I gave myself permission. It's really a beautiful state to be in. The feeling and power that you have makes you superhuman. You know your strength, and it's tough as hell to stay there. My goal is to get back to that state and remain there. I will tell you how I got there later in the book. For now, let's focus on the law of attraction and how to make it work for you. For the law of attraction to work, you must be forthright about what it is you want and start acting as if you already have what you desire. It is at this point that you create powerful energy that pulls to you exactly what you are asking for. Now, how does this look in your 3-D life? It appears that everything is happening to your benefit. You start meeting people that can take you closer to your desire. You find mentors, resources, and support from the strangest of places. Places that you might have already looked and thought that were dead ends. You feel vibrant and free and move with a creative spirit. You begin to act and believe that you have achieved it already. You feel good about your experience and start going further along. You begin to change your entire thought process around other areas of your life, which only pulls you closer in the magnetic field. The law is working. You understand that time is needed to manifest properly so you don't rush. By not rushing, you develop strong faith and trust. You are getting in flow. You develop a bulletproof mindset along the way. People start treating you differently. You begin to command respect and love. People naturally want to be around you because you are confident and happy all the time. You are moving away from negativity and moving closer to yourself. You develop stone cold strength. When you hear "no," you know that you are getting closer. That's how you begin to look at negative situations—you turn them into something positive. You attract new ideas and thoughts that only pull you closer to your overall goal. When you get there, finally—when your desire is materialized, guess what? You don't stop. You wish you only went for something BIGGER.

It's all in reach no matter if it's visible to the naked eye. We just need to focus the naked eye and concentrate on our inner power to achieve anything we want. You're going to come across many "gurus" and intellectuals that tell you their version of The Secret or The Law, but I am going to tell you, now, how to ensure you are not getting conflicting messages. Just listen to yourself. Feel it.

I too was an innocent bystander of many teachings that confused the hell out of me. I was up, then I was down; I was sideways and upside down. If you want to learn more about the law of attraction and spirituality and your own inner power, I will share with you my mentors on the subject. I don't have many. The one thing that I learned to develop was how to cut gurus off or turn them down for a while when I don't need them. Anyone that listens to a million and one sales tapes from all different people is a confused person. Or anyone that is practicing spirituality and adding new principles and newfound magic is confused. You have everything you have within you already. You just needed ONE person to guide you to yourself. You will see how easy spirituality is.

I encourage you to find one person who speaks to your soul and just invest in their material. The fastest way out of focus is taking on too many teachings that conflict with each other and require more your hours following them around that focusing on YOU. This book is about your journey and what it's going to take to get up, get out and get it done! I am just the middle (wo)man.

Let's go!

**Get Up, Get Out,
Get It Done!**

The Comfort Killers' manifesto is to get up, get out, and get it done! This is a no excuse, no holds-barred approach to attacking your day and going after your dreams in life, even if you have no idea what these dreams are yet. It begins with a rude awakening, a morning routine laced with personal development, and a slew of activity that'll drive the average person insane. This is how I conquered my fears over time, by building confidence in my work ethic and discipline.

Writing this book is a form of discipline. You want to know what else takes massive amounts of discipline, hard work, and consistency? Going to the same dead-end job for 30 years. That takes crazy work ethic, to wake up daily, hating every minute of it, but doing it daily—living for Friday nights and Holiday parties. Lately, I've felt underwhelmed at my place of employment; that is because I set a date to get the hell out of there. Day in and day out, we punch that clock without even questioning its mechanics and work on someone else's dreams and passions while ignoring our own passions and desires. I've worked for someone else for 18 years and I've had it. I been fired from four of the six jobs I've held in my lifetime, and I quit the remaining two. I am unemployable. I go into an establishment with the intention of having a good secure job to pay my bills and having a little fun on the side. The problem was I didn't get paid enough to cover basic living expenses, or I was bored out of my freaking mind. I was a rebel employee. Maybe you're the type too, the type of employee that never seems to follow directions and orders from someone else. I didn't want anyone telling me to do stuff, and I just hated the politics of climbing the ladder. I was different. There's millions just like me who for the life of them cannot figure out why they think differently. When you try to box them in, they resist. When you try to silence them, they speak louder. These characteristics were the beginning stages of defining what I would do in life. I couldn't go back to music, and I wasn't going to be someone who worked and retired broke without options.

The Manifesto:

Get up, get out, and get it done was the first thing I activated after converting myself from gambler to entrepreneur. It is the same manifesto that I live by today and will continue to live by until my days are ended on planet earth. It has worked for me, and I know implementing this ACTION concept will work for you too.

Get the F*CK Up!

It starts with you getting up. I mean, there's no other way of me explaining this process other than telling you, you got to get the F*CK up! Yes, with an exclamation point! When I didn't care about anything and my life wasn't fulfilling because I had 0 goals and aims, I woke up and lay there. I turned on the TV from the bed and chilled out for another hour or so until the tiredness wore off. It was damn dismal in the mornings. First off, I didn't have an alarm clock. My natural wakeup would be between 10 and 11 in the morning if I didn't have to work. When I worked, I would jump up because I was always late. I want you to notice something there. When I had to go to work, I would JUMP UP because I was late—which meant that I had the ability to JUMP UP for myself but never did. I was a slave JUMPING UP for an employer, another person, or a boss. How many times do you JUMP UP for other people, but you stay in bed for yourself?

That's the problem. We don't get going because we don't have the same push to do something we cannot see yet. That hasn't been created yet. That doesn't exist yet. We can't JUMP UP because there's no reason to. This is when you must do it. When we get up, we get up because we are the owners of our time, and we have set a schedule for ourselves because we have decided to take control back. Some of you reading may have tough work schedules and can't JUMP every day. My question to you is, what about your off days? What about any other time you are not working. "Oh, Stacy, you didn't have to work!" Please! I worked 40–50 hours a week and put in another 20–30 on my business right from the start. Right from jump street! There are 168 hours in a week. If 50 of those is for work and 56 hours are for sleep (depending on an average of 8 hours a night), then you are left with 62 hours for life. Let's subtract another 3 hours per day as a cushion for showering, getting dressed, cleaning, and eating. Now we are down to 41 hours left in the week. Ah, why not subtract another 2 hours for school or kids or commute per day? Now you are looking at 27 hours left in the week for life. What are we doing with our time? This is about getting up and getting your day started before the sun is up. This is about squeezing more hours out of the day that you are wasting. This is about JUMPING UP with enthusiasm and determination for a goal. You have 4 hours on average per day to get started on YOU. Here is a quote from Conrad Hilton, "to some degree, you control your life by controlling your time." Here is a quote by me: Get up, get out and get it done!

Get the F*CK Out!

After you jump up you are going to need something to do. I like writing and creating, so I did that. Then I started to create more and more. I noticed I was getting better at it. I was dedicated to making a name for myself. When you get out, you are getting out of your comfort zone by doing things you normally wouldn't do. You are learning a new language or watching programs teaching you some new skill. Maybe you're working on your body through fitness or maybe you're reading. Whatever it is you are doing, it will be unnatural and hard. You will become super distracted—you'll want to look at your phone, or worse, you'll feel the urge to go back to bed. Fight it. You already achieved the hardest part of this cycle, you got the f*ck up. The rest is downhill. This was my morning routine when I got totally uncomfortable:

1. Get out of bed immediately; do NOT think twice.
2. 20 sit-ups, 20 push-ups, and 20 jumping jacks.
3. Write down my goals and write in my journal.
4. Take a cold shower.
5. Listen to a morning meditation for 10 minutes.
6. Read 1 chapter or for 30 minutes.
7. Write an article.

This is all before 8 a.m. This all happened before most of America got out of bed. I would control my time and work on my personal development. It felt great and after some time, it was a discipline. Write a list of tasks you can fill your 2–3 hour block with. Maybe you want to write a book, record a podcast, or start a business. You can do it every day like clockwork, and just like clock-work, the universal law will support you.

Are you interested in knowing what all the universal laws are? There are 50 primary universal laws. The universe is perfectly balanced by natural and moral laws—work within them, be assured of eventual positive results. Work without them and find struggle.

If you want more information on these universal laws, invest time learning and observing each of them. My mentor Dick Stutphen will support your interest in this journey if you so choose to search.

1. Law of Harmony
2. Law of Reincarnation and Karma
3. Law of Wisdom
4. Law of Grace
5. Law of Soul Evolution
6. Law of Bodhisattva
7. Law of Vibrational Attainment
8. Law of Free Will
9. Law of One
10. Law of Manifestation
11. Law of Conscious Detachment
12. Law of Gratitude
13. Law of Fellowship
14. Law of Resistance
15. Law of Attraction
16. Law of Reflection
17. Law of Unconditional Love
18. Law of Magnetic Affinities
19. Law of Abundance
20. Law of Divine Order
21. Law of Attitude
22. Law of Threes
23. Law of Association
24. Law of Commitment
25. Law of Dissonance
26. Law of Experience
27. Law of Fearful Confrontation
28. Law of Group Consciousness
29. Law of Personal Return
30. Law of Activity
31. Law of Denial
32. Law of New Beginnings
33. Law of Compensation
34. Law of Psychometric Influence

I believe in sending individuals exactly what their hearts desired, and since you are attractive in the universe, you were most likely asking how people can increase their spirituality and abundance but had no clue where or how to start. Well, I've just played a key part in your universe and reality. You've attracted me.

I know that many reading this book are probably wondering to themselves what the hell is Stacy talking about, because they do not consider themselves spiritual. In fact, you don't subscribe to anything other than what you already know. Maybe that's the problem. Your mind-set also has its comfort zones, and your ego will react with opposition to anything that will teach it to relinquish control. Maybe you need more spirituality in your journey. Maybe you need to connect with your higher self. It's not space-y; it's consciousness, and you need tons of it if you want to start and grow any business. You need to develop the true you, the real you, because the person you've been dragging around your entire life doesn't represent love, abundance, and freedom. Take a month, meditate, and see what happens. I challenge you.

Get it Done!

My short manifesto is simple. We got up, then we got out of our comfort zones, and now we need to complete the cycle of getting it done. The reason why getting it done is important is because you will feel so good when the thoughts in your head are materialized in the physical universe, just like this book. Everything you complete is a product. An incomplete product cannot be used. Let's take a deeper look at this concept.

When you tie your shoes and they are nice and tied, it is a completed product. A half-completed product is not a product; it is an attempt. When we leave things attempted or half completed, we get confused, which causes doubt. When we ask ourselves a bunch of questions, we also get confused. Doubt turns into apathy, and then you're back to square one. The moment you start completing tasks and activities the full way through is when you'll start feeling good. You will notice you are happier and fulfilled. You will notice more energy surrounds you to get even more done. Therefore, an author rarely writes just ONE book. The athlete never wants to retire ... they love the feeling of completed activities and additional opportunities to do it all over again. Why? Because it feels good. This is my first book. I already have two more in mind. Matter of fact, I started both and it has been bothering me ever since. It has been nudging at me. If I completely quit, then I will never confront where a certain feeling of doubt is coming from. If you are in doubt, it is because you have incomplete projects around or half-finished products. Tie up the loose ends and get it done.

Another thing to note about products is that you can sell and exchange completed products for support, money, other products, or value. There's really no telling where you can stop. You write an article and complete it. It is a product on your website or blog. You can exchange it for support. People will read it and they will share it to their network. Now, you have value. You wouldn't be able to do that if it was still in draft mode. Think about the coffee shop in your neighborhood. What if every morning you went for a hot cup of coffee, the baristas turned to you and said, we didn't finish making the coffee. It's incomplete. There's no exchange. They don't get your dollars. You go to another shop that has completed products.

Whatever it is you intend to do, you must put everything into it. Even if it hurts, even if it's boring or time-consuming. You have got to finish that thing. If there is something that you are stopping, then you had better come to terms with why you are stopping this thing and end it knowingly. Do not even look back at it. It's super funny because, in the past, I would start and stop a bunch of things. I started/stopped a hip-hop newsletter. I started/stopped a mail-order clothing business. I started/stopped my music interest. I started/stopped a clothing brand. I would be lying to you if I didn't tell you that I learned this principle the hard way. I am appreciative of the experience I gained from each of my ventures of the past, but I sure fucked up my mindset by ingraining this start/stop quitter attitude in my subconscious over the years. Do you see why it was easier for me to attract challenges?

I am always being tested. And so are you—it's about learning.

Planners and Journals

There is no substitute for adopting The Comfort Killers Manifesto without documenting it. There just isn't. I am happy to say that I can open old journals and see exactly how far I've come on this journey. I can pinpoint where shifts took place and note where my mindset wasn't yet there. No one is going to tell YOUR story better than you. How could they? They didn't live it. And like it or not, your memory is going to fade faster than that old jean-jacket you have in the closet from the '90s. *Throw it out man.* That is why I recommend writing everything down. Supplement that with recording your voice too. Remember, this is for you and no one else. Get real with yourself and speak your mind. If you think you are not growing because you cannot see tangible results, just listen to yourself three months later. You are going to be amazed.

The first product that I created for my company were journals. I don't encourage writing about your girlfriend/boyfriend breakup stories in there, but I do implore you to write what matters. If love matters—go ahead and write about it. It's your story. Not mine.

Another area I had to step up in was scheduling my day to the T. If you do not have a planner go get one quick—the kind that breaks down the hours within the day. Schedule everything the night before. Just before you go to bed, your focus should be planning the next day. At first, I realized I was putting way too much in my daily planner, trying to knock out multiple projects throughout the day. It failed, as I was jumping around too much to accomplish one task fully. Now, I plan my day by projects. I would write my book during an entire 8-hour block and that would be it for the day other than a few phone calls for my business and posting a couple things to social media. This technique was more effective for me. In the past, I would write for 2 hours, then write articles for 1 hour, then schedule social media posts for 30 minutes, then block out 2 hours for updating the website, and 2 hours for sales, 1 hour for podcasting, etc. It was getting too hectic and disorganized. So now, I focus on one main objective for the day and inject small tasks that require a few minutes of my attention. What I notice now is that I am clearer and know precisely what I am going to do for the day. If something pops up, I am in control to say no or adjust my calendar to it.

Begin your journey with a journal. There's no coincidence that the spelling is similar.

When are you going to start? Are you going to wait another year complaining and blaming everyone else for your lack of ownership? If you haven't written anything in a journal before and don't even have one of those things—do this now.

1. Grab a sheet of paper.
2. Write the date at the top of the page.
3. Write down 3 things you are grateful for.
4. Write down what success looks like to you.
5. Write down 3 goals you have or new goals you want to achieve.
6. Write a date at the bottom of the paper.

Welcome to your new journal. Now keep track of your progress.

Move Towards Freedom

All your action should take you in one direction. Freedom. Why else would you be doing it? Some would say the money. That's freedom. Others may ask, more time with my children? That's freedom. Most would say, "I want to FIRE my BOSS!" That's mega freedom. Freedom is the umbrella for life. In life we've placed mental shackles around our wrists, feet, and neck. We were marionettes to people, places, and things. We never moved out from the towns we grew up in because we are afraid to be too far away from family. [Shackles clinking.] We are stuck in the same dead-end job for what seems like a lifetime. [Shackles clinking.] We cannot afford a vacation. [More shackles clinking.] We cannot travel. We can't say no to our parents. We sign up for community college and take one semester under the liberal arts program. We give up on our passions. We don't have enough money. We … we … we … never-ending shackles. Today is the day we are going to move towards freedom. Everything I just mentioned that shackles us can be eliminated in an instant. It's a mindset.

Have you ever heard the famous story about how they train elephants in the circus? Well, this story has everything to do with human freedom, so I will re-tell it again. When elephants are still small, they tie a rope around their neck and attach the rope to a pole. The baby elephants try to walk away naturally but are stopped by the rope each time they reach a certain distance. They try to push through it, pull through it and fight their way past the limits but eventually give up and figure that they just aren't strong enough to break free from their shackles. Soon after, they stop battling, they stop trying and just stay right where they are. They do this over and over to the baby elephant until it realizes it's no use and ultimately give up fighting for freedom. These elephants learn over time that when a rope is placed over their heads it is a signal that they should remain in the same place without resistance. They have lost their power to break free. They have become habituated to confinement. That is why you can walk into a circus and see a huge elephant with a rope around its neck attached to nothing at all. Even if the rope were attached to a pole or a tree or just about anything, these animals wouldn't break free of imprisonment.

True freedom is breaking free of a mindset that has a rope around your neck and is tied to nothing. It's tied to false beliefs, old ideas, and old ways of thinking. The rope (your mindset) has stifled your dreams. Someone said you couldn't do it, so you didn't. Someone said your personality doesn't typically "fit in," and you listened. You've listened to society label and discredit others, so you backed away. They said it takes money to make money, and you believed every word. Your parents said you were worthless, and you accepted. Your family were not the college types, so you passed on a scholarship to smoke weed. They said you were too short to play ball, so you played video games instead. Your teachers didn't give you a pass, so you took the failure. They laughed at you for wanting to join the drama club, so you didn't. You thought yourself an artist, but someone called your art a joke, then you stopped. Your mother said you needed to stay close to home and help take care of the family, and you gave up your goals for it. Your friends said your dreams were dumb, and you agreed. It's the rope. It has kept us in shackles for too long. The words of someone else should never dictate our feelings and actions. If you only knew how powerful you really were.

Over our entire lifetimes, we agreed to things we never really knew we had an option to disagree with because of societal pressures. I am a lesbian. People will look the other way from me because they've accepted and agreed to things in their lives people and media put on them. Even religion. Moving towards freedom really means moving toward your own free choice and free will. You can choose to stay in a situation that does not suit you and doesn't serve you due to its negativity and pain or you can choose to set yourself free of it and never look back. Look at the effect of domestic violence. We can never understand why someone would stay in that situation or keep going back to it. Is it because the rope that is around this person's neck is one that has been placed by someone in their past? We all have been victims of not moving towards freedom at some point in our lives. We all have an area of our life roped that we gave up on without end. There is no shame in it. We just must choose another path today.

Find it within you the strength to break free from false truths by the mere understanding that you are powerful and only you can live YOUR life. There is nothing holding you back but the choice you have made to remain in a debilitating situation. When I realized that it boils down to my attitude, I changed the course of my life to a positive one, understanding that each second I am given another opportunity to shift. Are you ready for the ultimate shift in life? Are you ready to take control back from this point forward? If the answer is yes, keep reading.

Find Beauty Everywhere

It's 2015. Winter. I must've just returned home from a quick casino loss because I remember how upset I was at myself yet again. Something was different about this day though. I remember I was fasting for a weekend to help me center my spiritual self. This was just a little after the water bucket challenge (who remembers that?). After losing my money and screaming to the heavens in the car, cursing and raging, it made better sense just to lay there and meditate. I was still using the aide of guided meditation programs off YouTube. There was one that I really showed more love than the others. I listened to it daily. I lay down and reflected on my day and reflected on how bad I wanted to change and how I wasn't happy with settling any longer. Something was different about that day; there was something amidst, an energy that I couldn't explain. To this day, I get goosebumps thinking about THAT day.

Everyone that meditates is thinking of absolutely nothing. True meditation is being focused on the internal self—without any focus on anything. If thoughts come up, you thank them and make them disappear. It's a rinse-repeat technique that builds major discipline as a byproduct. What would be going through my mind is, "Am I even doing this shit correctly?" How does one know if they've peaked? And to what end? I have gotten way better at silencing the mind, going on astral escapes and talking to my higher self through vibration and energy. I was addicted to meditation ... I wanted to climax, I needed to reach NIRVANAAAA!

If the Buddha experienced Nirvana after a lifetime then I experienced my version of Nirvana on THAT day. My eyes were closed. I was not moving. Guided mediation on in the background, nice and low. Suddenly, my eyelids glued shut as if I'd slipped into a deep coma. A white, luminescent, vibrational image appeared in my mind's eye, and I had a wave-like movement. I was trying to open my eyes. I couldn't. The waves kept going in and out in a 4-dimensional style—they pulsated rapidly and appeared to look like art.

Disclaimer: Words cannot describe how it looked in my mind. We are too linear of beings to comprehend and describe such beauty.

I'll try anyway. My eyes cemented shut. I could still sort of hear the meditation in the distance … it sounded far off. I was gone. At this point in the meditation, I completely slipped. That's when the scariest shit took place in my right ear.

First off, try to picture me there stuck—unable to move or open my eyes and seeing these internal, bright white waves flashing inside, then hearing a series of tones in my right ear, which were super loud. It was only in my right ear? It sounded like alternative frequencies, as if something was trying to communicate with me. Beeep … BEEEEP … BEEP BEEEP… BEEEEP. At this point, I was scared out of everything I knew existed. I knew I needed to relax to get whatever it was to stop, and so I did. I quieted down my energy and using my inside voice (because my mouth couldn't move) said, "please, stop," and instantly, I was able to come out of meditation.

When I got up, my entire body was one big goose bump. I jumped up, looked around the room, and asked myself, how long was I there? It was less than a minute but felt like 30 minutes. The guided meditation still playing in the background .. I quickly turned it off. What was strange was what took place inside and outside of me immediately following this event. I felt everything! I could feel the energy of everything. I felt the moon. I was extremely happy and didn't understand how. I felt unconditional love. I sat there for 20 minutes and poured my eyes out. I cried like a 2-year-old because I knew that I had shifted. Something happened that I couldn't explain, but something did shift. But why?

This is how I know we are powerful beings; this is how I believe we have all the tools and resources inside of us to succeed. I believe it because I feel it. It took me roughly 4–5 months for a complete body shift to take place. I couldn't sleep for months. Electrical energy or pulses kept rising from my feet to the top of my head. I would have all sorts of sensations and perceptions. I could absolutely feel everything. This is when a whole new world opened to me, a world that would put me on a new journey.

Most of you will probably not go through what I went through, but it's good to note how beautiful you are and how, right now at this moment, we have each other. You can sense things; you are free to use these powers you have within. **Try this:**

1. Lie down or sit up and close your eyes completely.
2. Do nothing—Do not move.
3. Feel what you want to feel.
4. Want to feel the energy of the table across the room. Bring it into consciousness and feel that shit.
5. It wants to be felt.
6. Feel random things.
7. Bring them into consciousness and feel.
8. Now try it on people. =)

We are now armed with a heightened sense of awareness. To become aware, one must perceive. You can perceive many things: thoughts, feelings, touch, point of view, emotion, love, infinity. Just sense. Remember, there are no right or wrong actions here. It's just you … you, the universe.

When I look out my window I don't just see houses, trees, the environment, people, or the sky. I perceive everything to be the reality that I created. When I see someone walk by, I say, "Oh, hey there, Thanks for stopping by at the perfect time for me to perceive you." I look at buildings, cars, and roadways as thoughts. These were created by me. I put them there, and I can take them out. As a Comfort Killer, you must begin a new mindset to take control of everything—not just the things that make sense but also the illogical, unthinkable, and unimaginable. Spirituality is a light topic because everyone is from spirit. We are just trying to make sense of all this heaviness. Our bodies, our troubles, and our pain. We collectively are going through life trying to figure this shit out. Some of us just perceive and understand more spiritually. These individuals are called old souls. I bet YOU are an old soul. Even if you fight it … trust you are. Shift your consciousness to the more innate self—you will know exactly what I am talking about when you make the decision to change.

Learning how to use your innate body to guide you is the key to self-mastery and to achieve anything you want in life. I want you to try something I've done throughout my journey to help me understand where to go next, who to talk to next, and what the answer is to questions that may change my life

The tool that you have is called "muscle testing."

I didn't create the concept of muscle testing. I am only sharing the wonders of using this self-technology. Muscle testing is something I picked up, tried, and applied through my studies. Now I store it in my mental toolbox for use anytime I need it. By using muscle testing you can be sure that you are getting answers from the subconscious mind—the human computer, recording everything that has ever happened to us in the now, the past, and previous lives. The subconscious mind knows exactly who we are, what's happening to us and how to heal ourselves, the innate and higher self. Skip this part if you don't want immediate answers to propel you into self-mastery. Amy B. Sher, author and energy specialist, summarizes muscle testing this way:

The body has within it and surrounding it an electrical network or grid, which is pure energy. Because energy runs through the muscles in your body, if anything impacts your electrical system that does not maintain or enhance your body's balance, your muscles will virtually "short circuit" or weaken (don't worry, only temporarily). Things that might have an impact on your electrical system are thoughts and emotions, foods, and other substances.

Using your muscles, we can find what events or emotions "weaken" or "strengthen" your body. This process is called applied kinesiology, but often referred to as "muscle testing." It's simply a really cool way we can ask your body questions and get clear answers – like a telephone to the subconscious mind.

From http://amybscher.com/getting-answers-from-the-subconscious-mind/

In late 2015, I took an assignment from the regional manager of the airline to help jumpstart a new city we just started operations in. The task was to help the two new supervisors transition into their new role by teaching our day-to-day responsibilities to ensure success. I was super excited to prove myself because up until that point I wanted to move up within the airline. I started as a ticket agent just four years before, and I had only one goal at that time. MOVE UP! After being a ticket agent for three months, I was promoted to lead, then within two years, to a supervisor. I was 100% dedicated to the company, its values, its culture—everything. I believed that it was where I needed to be. I spent more than three weeks in Albany training these two new supervisors. I missed Christmas and returned home on New Years Eve. I felt super blessed to know that there would be an opportunity to apply for a general manager position that I felt I was more than experienced for. After returning home, I started to prepare for the interview and gave it my all. I traveled to NYC fully prepared to crush this interview utilizing everything that I have experienced and learned in all my years, but especially the task that I completed in Albany. I thought I did great—they thought I wasn't the perfect fit. Before receiving the final verdict, I would muscle test 3-4 times a day telling myself: "I am the general manger of Philadelphia." I was shocked to find my body would lean backwards, signaling the answer was no. I cleared myself by asking "Am I clear?" and thinking, "My name is John," to ensure that the no was a no and the yes was a yes. Finally, I came to terms with the fact that I couldn't outsmart the energies of the universe within me. I wouldn't be getting the position I had worked so hard to prepare for. I never questioned the answers again.

"I look for the beauty in the universe and it shares with me the wonders within myself."
~ *Stacy A. Cross*

Life is Great.
Keep Producing.

During my interview with world famous salesman and multimillionaire Grand Cardone (NY Times Best Selling Author), I pulled out a small notepad and pointed to a quote that has helped me progress through the downs and struggles. I asked Grant to evaluate the quote and ask how it had helped him. The quote was "Production is the basis of morale" ~ L. Ron Hubbard. Grant alluded to the truth of the quote by solidifying its concept based on his own creations and how he never truly felt happy until he was at work, creating. I agree with this concept whole-heartedly. To accomplish a specific task will change you deeply. There's something that happens inside of you—it has to do with your endorphins, the feel-good chemicals that trigger positive feelings. At the end of the day, if you accomplish what you set out to do during the day, you feel great. That's success. Success isn't the accumulation of an entire lifetime as one looks back. There's tons of small successes you experience daily.

In contrast, I am not suggesting that you shouldn't have days where you disconnect and get your thoughts together or days you spend with your family just shooting the shit. That's important too. It's the entire scope of life that matters—health, wealth, and happiness. All of it matters. How are you producing with your loved ones? Are you taking the time (invested time) to be with your family, have a beautiful dinner, laugh, reminisce, or create new memories? How about your health production? Are you invested in working-out daily, producing more and more energy by changing your health habits? For me, it meant watching my sugar intake, hitting the gym, and adding more greens into my diet. It meant for me to detox and set a goal for losing weight. Creating financial free-dom is another form of production. When you constantly work on improving these 3 areas all at once, you begin to flow in harmony. Life just feels better. Solutions pop up out of nowhere in your head in the form of new ideas and easier routes. Some of my best ideas appear out of nowhere it seems when I am at work on myself.

Another important concept to note is "Creativity is the basis of morale." I firmly agree with this notion. When I was 13 years old, I started to write lyrics. I considered myself a rapper. All I ever did was consume music and create songs. I was heavily involved in the arts. I was a creative. It's a great feeling to add to the world something that was not there already. That is creation. Allowing others to love it, listen to it, look at it, read it, use it ... learn from it. These are all ways to add a piece of you to life. Some do not think about their legacy in their early years. I sure didn't think of legacy when I was growing up. But as I get older, it is something that I am more interested in. How can I leave myself here? How can I ensure that my name and personality withstand the ages? This book is the first step. Everyone must take the first step. It begins with realization. Setting goals is the very next step in the order of creation, and finally, we must produce.

If you don't know where to begin, this little trick may help you. Focus on the entire scope of life: Health, Wealth, and Happiness. Produce in these areas first and watch the miracles take shape. Make yourself do something every day to feel better about yourself and watch these feelings compound. It amazes me how much we are different. We bring something unique to the world, among billions of variations of humans. How special is that? You are you. The world needs you. The world doesn't need another Bill Gates, Oprah, Steve Jobs, Elon Musk, Grant Cardone, or anyone else you look up to or admire. The world needs you, and production will bring you happiness along with adding something beautiful to the world. Go create.

GET UNCOMFORTABLE

"You speak too low, and you walk too slow"
~ Stacy A. Cross

As we roll into the end of this book, I would like to share a story that'll help summarize this entire Comfort Killer Culture. It was the summer of 2014. I finally moved to a neighborhood I never thought I would live in. I was used to garden apartments with a balcony growing up. I never stretched for anything else, in fact; I thought I couldn't afford anything else.

I finally moved from Jersey to Philadelphia and became interested to live in a very active and entrepreneurial neighborhood. It was twice as expensive as the last place I lived in, but I found it was also twice as creative and it mirrored the lifestyle that I wanted. My landlord was a real estate investor, artist, philanthropist, entrepreneur, an all-around nice guy. One day I looked him up and learned that he had a few businesses on the block, so I decided I should learn from him by asking him to be my mentor. No strings. He agreed. We set a date and had a morning coffee at a local shop in the neighborhood. He then asked if I would like to come with him to see all that he did. I was totally ecstatic. At that time, I was working on my clothing brand, Preferred Classics; therefore, most of my questions revolved around that business specifically. The moment he stepped out of the coffee shop he was a bullet. Speeding through one store to the next, speaking about how it was acquired, how he designed it, and what he was planning to boost production. Then, he stopped and spoke to other people on the street. Everyone loved him, and it appeared everyone knew him. He would dash off again. All the while introducing me. All the while teaching me a valuable lesson. We then hopped in his truck and took off to his art studio. He put on a country song and explained the back story about its impact. I was in awe. He then hopped back in the truck, we went to his office—he needed to handle a few priority tasks. This was all within 1 hour after the last sip of coffee. It was then that I found out 3 important things.

1.   I walk too slow.
2.   I speak too low.
3.   I wasn't doing enough.

I walk too slow:

There's purposeful, directed, action-oriented walkers that take the stairs and move swiftly with intent, and then there are those who are not. I am very observant, and I noticed that 9 times out of 10, the types of people that move at lightning speeds throughout the day are action takers, wealthy entrepreneurs, or focused creators. I decided to walk 10% faster than I had. There I was, a young woman in relation to my mentor, who couldn't keep up. A light-bulb went off in my head. I said, "Wow, Stacy. You got to keep up with the winners or you will become a loser." I was pretty hard on myself, but I wanted to ensure that I was duplicating success. I didn't come from a family of entrepreneurs, nor did I have a rich dad to emulate. I had to decipher what were successful habits and what weren't for myself.

Do you know where you are going?

My travels recently brought me to York, PA. My team and I stopped in a local McDonald's for coffee and break-fast sandwiches to ease the morning growls. As soon as I walked in, I instantly knew that it wasn't a regular McDonald's. It was something different. The culture was different, and so was the energy of the place. Then my thoughts were verified when I made my order. The young guy behind the register wasn't just there to take my order.

He was also there to make me feel good. "Hello! Good morning, thank you for coming in. How can I help you?" We all looked at each other because we just knew. Then more actions by this entire staff made me a firm believer. Everyone was running from point A to point B, and it was a team effort. Every minute there was someone wiping down a table, smiling, and asking you if you needed anything. This McDonald's was a 5-star restaurant. I watched as one person's order was mixed up. Instead of the customer standing by the cashier's table, he was asked to have a seat and the correct order would be brought to him. The speed of these employees was fast, efficient, directed, and purposeful. I was instantly amazed by the culture.

So, how do you add purpose in your walk? Know what you are going to do—do it and don't waste any time. Watch people who drag their feet. These people obviously don't have anything going for themselves if they don't have energy about them to get going. How can these people finish projects? How can they make decisions? The next time you are in a public setting, like an airport—just watch people. Who is doing what? Observe the employees. Do they even look like they want to be there? I have learned from modeling the best—it becomes more evident each day that there are stark differences between the success-minded and the opposite.

A confident person walks upright, chin up, and in a hurry. Always got somewhere to go. Something important to do. Even if it's going to their car for something they forgot in the backseat.

Then it boils down to "What the heck are you going to say?"

You speak too low:

If I have to bend over, lean in, ask you to repeat your-self, say huh? Then there's good chance that you are speaking way too low. Am I the only one that notices this? I tell my employees that they must be confident in the way they walk and the way they talk. My mother is guilty of this. Our phone conversation usually ends in a hurry because she has diminished her voice so low that I think she is off the phone. I hang up and she calls me back cursing me out. Sorry, ma, you speak too low.

Having a quiet voice can hamper your social success. In the past, I caught myself speaking way too low for the environment I was in. I was asked a question, and instead of being confident and assertive, I retreat by speaking in a soft tone. The person usually ended up wondering what the hell I said, or worse, saying "HUH?" I hated this so much I knew it was time to change. I worked on myself by speaking up, being direct, and being bold in my voice. People naturally are attracted to those that are able to communicate well. So, I focused on leveling up my com-munication skills, which has helped me tremendously in getting support by being able to get my point across.

Are you a low speaker? Do people constantly ask you to repeat yourself? Take a self-assessment. Get honest and start making changes.

I wasn't doing enough:

Walking around with my mentor for an hour made me realize that I wasn't doing enough. Sure, I had a fulltime job, a clothing business headquartered in Jersey, and a fulltime personal development plan. I still knew that somehow, I wasn't on purpose. It was because a lot of my time was also spent in the casino—pounding away at slots and getting upset with myself. I was always on this roller coaster. It can feel like you are never doing enough when you are not doing the right things, the most ethical things. It will haunt you. In order to get past this, I decided to do the opposite of everything that was not serving my goal. Eliminating my gambling addiction was pretty tough. I got uncomfortable owning up to the fact that I wasn't living right. I then got uncomfortable filling the time I used to gamble with creating a new business.

Get around other people trying to do better things.

I started going to seminars. Well, I went to two. One was a real estate investing seminar and the other was a wealth mindset seminar. On the first day of the second seminar I'd ever been to, I walked out and started The Comfort Killers. I knew exactly what I needed to do—I needed to the opposite.

Move into fear.

Here's news for you. We are all afraid. Show me a man that is fearless, and I will show you a dead man or someone that is pretending to not feel the emotion of impending danger, pain, or threats—both real or imagined—heading his way. I like to use fear to move me towards what I am afraid of instead of letting it push me away. Inaction is a result of fear overpowering an individual. In order to grow, we must move towards the very thing that has got us shaking in our boots. I was once afraid of speaking in public. Every chance I got, I ran away from the opportunity to hone in on my communication skills. I thought the worst of my vocabulary, speech, nuances, and accent. I believed that I was a fumbler of words. Podcasting has helped me tremendously overcome this fear. The more I spoke, the better I got. It wasn't long until

I was promoted into a role where speaking to small to medium sized groups would be an everyday thing, and I couldn't make an excuse to retreat into comfort. My fear has made me lots of contacts and connections, and it allowed me to form new relationships both inside of business and out. Move into fear. Whatever has got you scared will also make you grow. One day at a time.

I wrote this book to show you that you have everything you need to succeed in the palm of your hands. Grit is a quality I picked up along the way. I was gritty when many people doubted what this would become. There was no doubt that I had to focus on the task at hand to make my life better. There was not a single doubt in my mind that I would outperform my own self and set even bigger goals. People recognize action; they respect it—there's no other choice for them.

Change Your Attitude, Then Aptitude.

Our (American) workforce is being infiltrated. Baby boomers have retired off to sunny Florida and took with them the workmanship that had been instilled by their parents and grandparents. I've noticed the golden shift inside and outside of organizations. This shift has everything to do with attitude and aptitude. I just so happened to catch a radio show on my commute home where a generation X caller spoke about millennial employees he had to manage and train. He sounded very upset at the way these employees handled work responsibilities. It appeared that they wanted everything handed to them, without the effort or willingness to take on additional responsibilities. At first, I completely agreed with this caller because I was dealing with similar issues at my job as a supervisor. Faces would be mad if they were required to stay even just 30 minutes extra to support the operation. People would have silly arguments and disputes about things that did not and would not ever move them forward in life. Me personally, I see it as an advantage for those millennials reading this book—or listening to my courses. There's a place in the world for you, especially since everyone wants to sit, chill, watch Netflix, and cry about everything that didn't go their way.

I started writing another book: *How to Develop Leadership Qualities in An Entry Level Position* because I know at a time like this, it will be a necessity to learn about different ways to exceed even your own expectations and goals in the workplace. I could have easily fallen off course and rode the average wave, and I am telling you, those are the people that are "retiring" or "quitting" every year. The same ones that have settled for less. They have not done anything to further the advancement of themselves and the company.

You are probably thinking, why should I care about a 9 to 5? Well, I believe in "you need food on your table and clothes on your back." You must do what you gotta do to survive. Don't try to be like these cornballs out here just to look cool. Hone your skills. Take all the training that is offered. Sit with your leader; ask for advice on how to move up. GET MORE MONEY. Move if necessary. Take on new roles and hats. Learn everything. Get better than everyone. That's how you win. You must play the game and outsmart everyone else. It may mean that you have ZERO work friends and skip the holiday parties or happy hours. Believe me when I say, you must get serious about winning and expanding. Even before you start a business, any business, you must lay foundational discipline and leadership qualities first.

Comfort Killers are everywhere—at work, in school, in gyms, libraries, onstage, and flying the friendly skies. They are everywhere. If you are ever in doubt, just take a good look in their eyes ... and tell them to remain uncomfortable.

I am Stacy A. Cross, and there is no "E" in my name! Until next time.

P.S.

Are You In? Join The Comfort Killers now – www.thecomfortkillers.com

Don't miss out on the opportunity to make this book come to life by signing up to my Building Blocks to Success 30-Day Program now! ~~($997.00~~ FREE for YOU!)

NOTES

www.ingramcontent.com/pod-product-compliance
Lightning Source LLC
Chambersburg PA
CBHW021242090426
42740CB00006B/660